THE

BAAL

CONSPIRACY

THE
BAAL
CONSPIRACY

AN EXPOSÉ OF EVERYDAY IDOLATRY

AL TRUESDALE

BEACON HILL PRESS
OF KANSAS CITY

ISBN 978-0-8341-2530-8

Cover Design: Lindsey Rohner
Interior Design: Sharon Page
Cover photo: Tobias Helbig

Library of Congress Cataloging-in-Publication Data
Truesdale, Albert, 1941-
    The Baal conspiracy : an exposé of everyday idolatry / Al Truesdale.
        p. cm.
    ISBN 978-0-8341-2530-8 (pbk.)
    1. Idolatry. 2. Christian life—Nazarene authors. I. Title.
    BV4627.I34.T78 2010
    241'.3—dc22

2010012313

I wish to express appreciation to Carole Cashman, Nancy Clapham, and Jim Cato for reading and critiquing the manuscript. They made many helpful suggestions.

Jim Andrews helped refine the title. Thank you, Jim.

As with anything I write, my wife, Esther, has patiently and persistently critiqued each draft. She has a special way of saying, "You're not there yet; back to the drawing board!" This book is lovingly dedicated to Esther.

"The heart of the biblical understanding of idolatry running through the whole Bible is that we take on the characteristics of what we worship. We become what we worship."

—G. K. Beale, *We Become What We Worship*[1]

Cast each false idol from its throne,
The Lord is God, and he alone:
to God all praise and glory.

—Johann Jakob Schütz (1640-90)

CONTENTS

THE SCHEME

Sprawled like a rag at the feet of Pompey's statue, Julius Caesar bled profusely from multiple dagger thrusts. Thirty-four, thirty-five, and the deed was done. Sixty members of the Roman Senate had successfully conspired to kill the man they thought was abusing power and spoiling Rome. As many conspirators as possible plunged their daggers into Caesar. Having ignored an ominous warning not to enter the Hall of Pompey, the great Julius Caesar died (44 BC), a victim of one of Western history's most famous conspiracies.

Conspiracies can happen in amazing forms. In late 2007, court documents charged that the Canadian divisions of Nestlé, Mars, Hershey, and other candy companies had conspired to fix prices in that country's annual billion-dollar chocolate bar industry. Ottawa court documents alleged that senior executives of the chocolate companies had met secretly at coffee shops, restaurants, and conventions to fix prices. The conspiracy was led by ITWAL Ltd., a major Canadian food distributor. Charges spilled beyond Canada. Lawsuits were soon filed in the United States. Early in 2008, the German Federal Cartel Office raided the offices of seven leading chocolate companies searching for documents.

These stories illustrate how conspiracies can have national or international importance. Conspiracies may scheme to kill opponents, overthrow governments, or embezzle multinational corporations. As astonishing as human conspiracies are, one conspiracy dwarfs them all—the Baal Conspiracy. This conspiracy carries cosmic significance, for it affects every corner of God's creation. It receives its name from the pagan god of fertility who subverted the faith of Israel and Judah. Baal worship was the dominant religious system the children of Israel encountered when they entered Canaan. Its seductive power was deadly.

The goal of the Baal Conspiracy is to defeat God. The field on which it unfolds is the universe in general and the people of God specifically. It works to achieve its aims by eroding the relationship between God and his people. It attempts in every way possible to undercut God's claim upon the undivided love and worship of those who call him Lord. The Conspiracy plays upon our blind spots. All of us are vulnerable.

The chief conspirator is Satan. His coconspirators are "Legion" (Luke 8:30). Like all conspiracies, success relies on deception. The Baal Conspiracy does not enlist armies of atheists who can mount frontal attacks on God. Its intended targets can recognize and fend off such tactics. The current response by Alister McGrath and others to books such as Richard Dawkins's *The God Delusion* and Christopher Hitchens's *God Is Not Great* demonstrates this. For example, in *Dawkins' God: Genes, Memes, and the Meaning of Life,* McGrath easily exposes Richard Dawkins's distorted understating of God.[2]

The Baal Conspiracy "flies below the radar" used to intercept militant atheism. To achieve its goal, it tries to enlist the people of God—those of us who sit in church on Sunday morning or Saturday night—as its agents.

God cannot be destroyed. But the Conspiracy's success does not require that. If Satan can get us to insert inferior interests and motives into our worship, then the Conspiracy will accomplish its goal. It will have diverted and diluted our worship. This amounts to requiring God to share his deity with other things. It boils down to adding gods to our worship. The catalog of "other things" is endless. Shared worship was what Baal worship by the people of Israel was all about.

The devil knows what God has said: "I am the LORD, that is my name; my glory I give to no other, nor my praise to idols" (Isa. 42:8). God doesn't share his deity with any other. But if Satan can achieve "shared deity" in the lives of those who profess to love God, he will have added success to his ancient scheme. The affirmation "Lord of all" will have been subverted.

All of this can happen unwittingly on our part. But it happens nonetheless. What better way for Satan to achieve his goal than for us to do his bidding without realizing it?

The Baal Conspiracy is agile. Its nature and strategy never change. However, its tactics shift from one era, one culture, and one circumstance to another. It has an inexhaustible wardrobe of disguises. We should never underestimate Satan's ability to deceive. He is a talented master of the craft. Prince of Darkness is another of his names. His résumé includes a long history of using the language of heaven to achieve the aims of hell.

The Conspiracy can be compared to a virus. It thrives by invading and feeding upon host cells. Battling and overcoming the Conspiracy in one's own life and in the Church requires rigorous honesty, discernment, and humility.

The twentieth-century German martyr Dietrich Bonhoeffer distinguished between "cheap grace" and "costly grace."[3] For Christians to be armed for battle against the Conspiracy they must become students of "costly grace." They must submit to mastery by the Holy Scriptures. The Scriptures show us how the Conspiracy functions and how God's people should confront it.

A most remarkable and discerning opponent of the Baal Conspiracy was Elijah, the ninth-century prophet who preached to the Northern Kingdom (Israel). In Elijah's day, Baal worship passed for advanced agricultural science. It explained fertility—why people, cattle, and seed reproduce. It told farmers how to maximize success as planters and breeders of livestock. Baal also offered the key for success in everyday life. What could be wrong with that? "Everything," Elijah answered. Baal worship subtly undercut the first and second commandments by personifying and then worshipping features of God's creation that should have prompted undivided worship of him as the sole Creator and Sustainer.

To understand the Conspiracy as it functioned in Israel in the ninth century BC, we will be instructed by a farmer journeying to Mount Carmel for a battle between Yahweh and Baal. In succeeding chapters, we will observe diverse ways Satan conspires to drive wedges between God and his people.

The devil is a confirmed recycler. Even today he disguises and recycles all forms of the Conspiracy we find in the Bible. He does not discard effective tools just because they are old.

Satan's conspiracy is this book's uniting theme. Each chapter is set within different historical periods of the Bible. Both actual and fictional characters narrate the stories. Each chapter is true to its historical context.

A section titled "Getting Ready to Hear" introduces every chapter but the last. It provides a brief history, insights about characters, pertinent scripture references, and a hint regarding the form of the Conspiracy about to be presented.

Recognizing the Conspiracy is not enough. We must have resources for defeating Satan's scheme and for worshipping God alone. All those resources are available in Christ. The Epistle to the Ephesians provides an excellent summary of the riches our Lord has made available through the Holy Spirit. In the final chapter we will explore Ephesians and learn how to be armed with "a spirit of wisdom and of revelation in the knowl-edge of [Christ]" (Eph. 1:17, RSV).

A timeline is located at the end of the book.

A WORD OF CAUTION

Jesus told a story about two men who went to the temple to pray—one a Pharisee, the other a tax collector (Luke 18:9-14). The Pharisee was quite confident about his purity and inno-cence. He boasted about the differences between himself and the tax collector. The tax collector on the other hand would not even lift his eyes to heaven. He prayed, "God, be merciful to me, a sinner!" (v. 13).

In each of the following chapters we will have opportunity to read as a Pharisee or as a tax collector. Jesus concluded his parable by saying that only the tax collector went home recon-ciled to God.

THE
BAAL
CONSPIRACY

Getting Ready to Hear

(Chapter 1)

The united kingdom of David and Solomon split apart in 922 BC (the exact date is debated). The Northern Kingdom became known as Israel; the Southern Kingdom as Judah. Samaria was the capital of Israel; Jerusalem the capital of Judah. Israel fell to the Assyrians in 722 BC.

Worship of the pagan fertility deity Baal—who took different names and forms in the ancient Near East—was a constant threat to both kingdoms. Baal worship was an essential part of the more sophisticated culture the seminomadic Israelites had encountered upon entering Canaan in the thirteenth century BC. Archaeological excavations show that early Israelite life was crude when compared to the sophisticated, aristocratic culture of Canaan.

The subtle and powerful attraction of the Baal fertility cult—especially in the North initially—can hardly be overstated. The mythical stories and practices associated with Baal explained and guaranteed the fertility required for successfully growing crops, raising livestock, and producing human offspring. Baal worship revolved around the cycles of nature. As we shall see, it intimately involved those devoted to it.

One of its most prominent supporters was Jezebel, wife of King Ahab, who reigned over Israel from approximately 869 to 850 BC. During Ahab's reign, the prophet Elijah battled the erosion of Israel's faith brought on by Baal worship. While worshipping Baal, the people also "worshipped" Yahweh. The conflict between Elijah and the priests of Baal reached its climax on top of Mount Carmel.

At stake in that contest was the very center of Hebraic faith. Is the Exodus God the Lord of all, or is he not? Does he share deity with other gods, or does he not?

Let's travel with a fictional Israelite farmer and his neighbors as they journey to Mount Carmel. He will explain the attraction of Baal worship and why he and his neighbors mixed the worship of Yahweh with the worship of Baal.

This chapter uncovers the fundamental nature of the Baal Conspiracy.

The pertinent scriptures are Judg. 2:11-15; 1 Kings 18; Ps. 65:5-13; and Zech. 10:1-2. Study Solomon's contributions to the corruption of Israel's faith (1 Kings 11:1-13). Judah was not far behind the Northern Kingdom in adopting Baal worship. See the judgment in 1 Kings 14:21-24. Gomer, who was the wife of the prophet Hosea, personified the Northern Kingdom's incorrigible lust for Baal (Hos. 1:1—2:13).

— 1 —

THE TROUBLER

I see that you are a visitor to these parts. My fellow villagers and I are journeying westward toward Mount Carmel. People from other towns and villages have come. All of us wonder why the *Troubler* has summoned us. Walk awhile with us. I will tell you about my family, my neighbors, and our way of life.

I am Jubal—a ninth century BC small farmer. I live in Israel's highlands. Our village lies within walking distance of my fields. Stone walls mark off each farmer's land. My fields—which actually belong to Yahweh—are hilly and rocky. They have been in my family for generations, part of what our clan received when our ancestors settled in Canaan. Our village forms an enclosed circle. It is located north of Gath-hepher—about thirty kilometers west of the Sea of Chinnereth. Cisterns hewn from the rock, and a nearby stream, normally provide our water. I say, "Normally," for both sources are now dry.

Like some other families in my village, three generations (soon to be four) live under my roof: my aged parents; my wife and I; and an orphaned niece, two unmarried daughters, and two sons and their wives. "Crowded," you say? That is just our way of life.

As you might expect, my aged parents are not able to travel.

My country is Israel, the northern part of what was once the united kingdom of David. But shortly after Solomon's death, the kingdom broke apart. Two countries with two different kings, capitals, and places of worship resulted. But this history is of minor importance when compared with my urgent need to make a crop, feed my family, and pay the king's taxes.

I am sure you can understand why failure would bring disaster. No national "social safety net" exists to break my fall.

JUST "MAKING A LIVING"

Life is hard. Everyone works for family survival—men with their assigned tasks and women with theirs. We work from sunrise to sunset. In seasons of fieldwork, those of us who work the fields and orchards leave home early enough to arrive at daybreak. We return home at nightfall. Sometimes we stay in the fields overnight.

In good times, my neighbors and I produce a surplus—partly because we have learned to adapt to inhospitable conditions. We have cleared forests to gain more land and built terraces to collect rainwater. But even when we accumulate surpluses, King Ahab levies heavy taxes to support his court and building projects.

Our agricultural year begins with plowing, and sowing wheat, barley, and millet. This happens from late October to late December. From late December to late February comes the late sowing of legumes and planting vegetables, such as cucumbers and marjoram. In March, we hoe weeds to be used as hay. From the spring equinox to late April, we harvest barley. This signals the beginning of ingathering. At the beginning of this period, we celebrate Passover. From late April to late May, we harvest wheat and measure grain. This season ends with the celebration of Pentecost. We harvest grapes and make wine in June and July. Summer fruit such as figs, pomegranates, and dates are harvested from late July to late August. The season of ingathering ends with two months of olive harvesting from late August to late October. The great Feast of Tabernacles comes at the end of the olive harvest.

Then, we begin again.

A few draft animals and some black goats and fat-tail Awassi sheep round out my sources of income and food.

Rain! We are desperately dependent upon regular rains. No watered soil, no harvest. No harvest, eventual starvation, for our storage is limited. It's that simple. Because our river valleys are not suited for large-scale irrigation, my neighbors and I carefully maintain stone terrace walls for retaining water moisture and soil. Rainfall peaks December through February. Normally we can expect about fifteen inches of rainfall per year. There is little room for error.

I should mention that I am fortunate to live in the North and not in the South where the climate is less favorable. The South is a semiarid region where rainfall is negligible. I understand why there is a difference between rainfall in the North and South. I know why my neighbors and I usually enjoy plentiful crops of citrus, olives, figs, and grain. The reason is that we live by an agricultural plan that, until recently, brings the rains. Our kinsmen in the South are much less observant of the plan. So they must bear the negative consequences.

The plan was working quite well until the *Troubler* showed up and began to interfere. In God's name, he began to condemn the plan as sinful. The whole country has been thrown into turmoil. The king and queen are furious. Word is out that Queen Jezebel wants the *Troubler* killed. And what she wants she usually gets.

ORTHODOXY ON DEMAND

I think you will be impressed by our support for the shrines at Dan and Bethel. My neighbors and I regularly worship the God of the patriarchs and Moses. Our rituals are quite impressive. Unlike the people in the South, who have only one temple, the North has two shrines for Yahweh. Jeroboam, our first king, established these religious centers. His purpose was to bolster his kingdom and keep his subjects from worshipping in Jerusalem. Going to Jerusalem would imply the Southern Kingdom's superiority. And it would drain precious money from the North. So to provide religious legitimacy for his kingdom, Jeroboam built one shrine at Dan in the northern sector and another at Bethel on the southern border. Jeroboam also established a priesthood that claimed descent from Moses—not from Jerusalem.

Like our kinsmen in Judah to the south, we regularly participate in the worship of Yahweh. We fulfill three pilgrimage festivals God requires. The spring Feast of Unleavened Bread in which we celebrate our exodus from Egypt comes first. We associate this festival with Passover. It happens at the beginning of the barley harvest. Seven weeks later we celebrate the Feast of Weeks, or Pentecost. This takes place during the wheat harvest. Then in later October we celebrate the Feast of Ingathering, or Tabernacles.

During the festivals, my family and I purify ourselves as ritual requires. Nothing goes unattended. We renew our covenant with Yahweh. As we make our way to Dan or Bethel, we do a lot of singing and dancing—accompanied by stringed instruments. What a glorious time the festivities offer—much anticipated and now fulfilled.

There's much more. The priests often require us to fast so as to humble ourselves before Yahweh. Added to that, the priests regularly present our burnt offerings on the altars at Dan and Bethel. I know exactly how to contribute to the sacrifices. Believe me, there are offerings, offerings, offerings!

As you can see, over the years my neighbors and I have accumulated an enviable record of observing holy days and festivals. We are pleased. God must be also. At least that's what we always believed before the *Troubler* arrived. He has begun to label us—in fact, almost all of Israel—"idolaters." No one escapes his attacks! Even King Ahab, Jezebel, and the priests are targets of the *Troubler's* condemnation. Given our admirable religious credentials and the effort we put into pleasing the Lord, it's hard to imagine a more ridiculous accusation.

Speaking of trouble—for almost three years, neither dew nor rain has come. For three planting cycles there have been no crops in the fields and no fruit on the vines. Our surpluses are nearly exhausted. Starvation stalks the land. Most of our animals have perished. Those that survive are little more than haunted shadows. No one, not even Ahab's household, has been spared. Even Ahab has been seen foraging for grass to feed his horses and mules.

How disruptive! All our problems began with that *Troubler.*

WHY THINGS GROW

Earlier, I said I know why things grow. Let me explain.

Before the drought, when things were going well, one of the most amazing events of the entire year was watching seeds transform into sprouts, sprouts into tender stalks, and tender stalks into a harvest of wheat, barley, and so on. But first, the rains had to come. Upon that mystery *all* life depended.

Amazing indeed. But my neighbors and I understand the mystery of fertilization—why rains come and seeds eventually sprout. We know how to make sure it all unfolds on time. The explanation and all it involves are the agricultural science of our day. We understand the story behind the science and faithfully reenact it year after year as we plant and breed.

At heart, the explanation for the rhythm of the seasons and the mystery of fertility revolve around the god Baal. He is lord of the storms and rains. He sends the rains that fertilize the seeds. Baal sparks all fertility, thus assuring our survival and prosperity. I have been told that "Baal" means "lord," "master," or even "husband." Different names are used in different places. We call him Baal of the Heavens and Rider of the Clouds because he controls rain and storms.

But you need to understand that Baal doesn't just wake up one day and decide to send the rains. The science is much more complex than that. Baal's wife, Astarte (sometimes we call her Asherah), plays a strategic role too. Here is how it all works.

Long ago, the god El and his wife gave birth to many gods, one of whom was Baal. In time, Baal defeated the other gods and became the most powerful. Some of the gods Baal had to defeat were Yamm (god of the sea) and Mot (god of death). Baal was assisted by his sister Anath (goddess of war) and Astarte (goddess of the earth and fertility). Victorious, Baal could now control the threatening sea and storms. He could bring annual renewal and fertility to the earth.

But each year, Mot (god of the underworld) kills Baal. Anath finds and buries Baal's body. The time in which Baal is dead is winter. Later, Anath kills Mot. Baal is now free to rise from the dead and escape the underworld. He returns to his palace on Mount Saphon and prepares to water the thirsty ground, fertilize the seed, and restore abundance to the earth. This part of Baal's life parallels the beginning of spring.

Do you understand my explanations so far?

Baal doesn't do all of this by himself. His wife, Astarte, helps him. Each year, after being rescued by Anath, Baal and Astarte engage in sexual intercourse. Houses in my village contain small shrines that display figurines of Astarte. She is nude and usually pregnant. Her hands support and hold out her large breasts. This symbolizes the fertility she offers.

My neighbors and I know that if Baal succeeds in impregnating Astarte, the rains will come and the fields will eventually surrender their yield. Our families, cattle, and oxen will eat and live for another year. Surpluses will be stored and taxes paid. But if Astarte doesn't become pregnant, or if Baal is angry with us, the rains will not come. There will be no crops in the fields and eventually no cattle in the stalls. It's that simple.

It is important for you to understand that success is not left to chance. My neighbors and I—all Israel—play an indispensable role in making sure Baal becomes sexually aroused and that Astarte becomes pregnant. On a seasonal basis, the adult males and females in my family—along with my neighbors—go to sacred places dedicated to Baal and Astarte. These are usually groves in high places. Nearby there are upright stones that symbolize the male sex organ. Sacred poles called Asherim also form part of the shrines. They symbolize Astarte. Under priests' cautious eyes, we sacrifice sheep and bulls in the shrines.

Next, the other males and I engage in sexual intercourse with sacred prostitutes. We do this to make sure that Baal will be aroused and have sexual intercourse with Astarte. While we are doing that, our wives and the other women have intercourse with male prostitutes. They do this to assure Astarte's pregnancy. Unless both things happen, the earth will not be fertilized, our wives will bear no children, and our animals will bear no offspring. Life rides on our diligence and success.

If our worship succeeds and Astarte becomes pregnant, Baal will send the rains and the earth will bear fruit. Life will be good for another year.

With so much riding on our efforts, we don't need to be reminded to fulfill our sacred duties. Is it any wonder that as we worship Baal, we are often seized by frenzied excitement?

Baal and Astarte are everywhere. In addition to the shrines in our homes, we maintain local and regional hilltop shrines. Conveniently, while at a shrine, we can worship Yahweh, Baal, or Astarte—or all three at once. At least one of our shrines contains an image of a female lover for Yahweh. Rigid distinctions between Yahweh, Baal, and Astarte are unnecessary—even counterproductive.

Some time ago, our science received a boost when King Omri arranged a marriage for his son Ahab. Omri arranged with Ethbaal, King of Tyre (in Phoenicia), for Ahab to marry Ethbaal's proud daughter—Jezebel. The marriage strengthened the relationship between Israel and powerful Phoenicia. Jezebel proved to be a zealous evangelist for her Phoenician deity—Baal-Melkart. She also brought along a large number of Baal prophets and supported them from Israel's public treasury.

King Ahab demanded that I help build a Baal temple in Samaria, the capital city. The temple was for Jezebel's use. Others helped the Baal priests build an altar for Astarte and an image of her. Unchecked by Ahab, Jezebel then tried to destroy all the prophets of Yahweh. She even tore down Yahweh's altars.

DIVINE COMPARTMENTS

If you wonder how we can worship the God of Moses and Baal at the same time, I can explain. It is all a matter of respecting boundaries. Some parts of life belong to Yahweh, and some to Baal. In some parts of life we worship Yahweh; in others we worship Baal. A long time ago, maybe as far back as when our ancestors settled the land, the distinctions were established. They have worked quite well—that is, until that *Troubler* arrived. He has thrown the compartments into confusion.

Here's how all the pieces fit together. Yahweh—the God of Moses and Aaron—is the God of power. As the Divine Warrior, Yahweh marches at the head of heavenly armies. He fought and defeated Pharaoh. He parted the sea and led the Israelites through the desert. Later, Yahweh divided the Jordan River and brought our people into Canaan. This powerful God broke down Jericho's walls and scattered the Canaanites. He is a fearful warrior and the miracle-working God of the desert. In times of national threats from our enemies, Yahweh can be counted on.

But that has little to do with the everyday affairs of life such as receiving rain, growing grapes, and paying the bills. We need a god who can bring order to the small stuff also.

Our ancestors were nomads when Joshua led them into this land. They knew almost nothing about how to make this stingy land productive. They could raise sheep but not melons and barley. They didn't understand the cycles of nature and the fertility of the soil. They had to learn from the Canaanites. That's how they found out about Baal's importance. After a few failed crops, the Canaanite explanation for agricultural success began to make a lot of sense. It dawned on our ancestors that Yahweh is the powerful God of the desert and battles. But some other god must ensure fertility. And that's where Baal comes into the picture. He is the farmers' and fathers' indispensable friend. Without his aid, we die.

So, you see, in Israel we have successfully divided the regions of life between Yahweh and Baal. If we carefully maintain the boundaries, neither deity will have reason to complain.

THE TROUBLER

But the *Troubler*—a prophet of Yahweh named Elijah— howls endlessly that our arrangement between Yahweh and Baal is blasphemous. He dismisses Baal as just a creation of sin and ignorance. He shouts that we and our ancestors have bought a lie; Yahweh will not comfortably share deity with other gods as the Baal priests claim. We are gross idolaters, the *Troubler* charges. The ridiculous message he spreads—that Yahweh must be *Lord over everything* and that Baal is *no god at all*—strikes us as unhinged from the obvious. Heeding him would leave us with no wheat, no lambs—nothing!

The *Troubler* declares there must be no compartments, no boundaries, in our worship of and trust in Yahweh. He preaches that Yahweh is Lord, not only of the desert but of agriculture as well; not only of "exodus" but of "settlement." *He is Lord of all life*—even the cycles and rhythms of nature. The whole earth, the *Troubler* proclaims, is the Yahweh's. He alone sends rain and causes the crops to grow. He alone provides the harvest. Confronted by such words, no wonder people shake their heads in disbelief. Jokes about the *Troubler*'s sanity abound. When we get to Mount Carmel, I plan to ask him, "How many crops have you planted? How many sheep have you bred?"

Elijah accuses us of worshipping things Yahweh created. "Worship and serve Yahweh only," the *Troubler* cries in towns and villages. To top it all, he actually accuses us of being dupes in an ancient conspiracy. No wonder Queen Jezebel wants to sever his head from his body.

THE GREAT CONTEST

We have arrived.

Today, the top of Mount Carmel is covered. Men, women, and children are trying to find a place to stand or sit amid the rocks. Children's faces seem to reflect the apprehension we feel. We still don't know why we are here.

The prophets of Baal are present. What colorful ritual robes they wear—just what we expect from men of such confidence and importance. The rest of us look shaggy by comparison.

In the distance, I see a patch of the Mediterranean Sea framed by two mountain peaks. Facing north, in the distance a bay sparkles before me. Stretching out to the southeast lays the parched Jezreel Valley. Such contrasts!

Suddenly, a cry of alarm goes up from the crowd. "Look," people yell, and point to a strange figure standing atop a knoll. Someone cries out, "It's that prophet! That's him!"

I quickly turn and fix my gaze upon the *Troubler*. How did he get here? I am startled, for he is a mighty frightful sight. He is short and skinny. His shaggy hair falls upon a loose-fitting coat made of rough animal hair. A piece of leather forms his girdle. I say to myself, "Someone should feed him."

Then, a thunderous voice too strong for its frame takes command of the scene. "It's time for a showdown between Yahweh and Baal this day and in this place," the *Troubler* shouts. "Either Yahweh *or* Baal will be Israel's God, but not both. It's time to determine who is Lord of your daily lives as well as your religious feasts."

The questions I meant to ask melt away. I begin to suspect that a contest of epic proportion is about to happen. The *Troubler* has taken charge.

Before anyone can protest, the *Troubler* issues the rules. "We will prepare one sacrifice for Yahweh and one for Baal. The one who sends fire to consume his sacrifice will be the true God. The God who breaks the drought will be the Lord of nature."

The contest seems humorously lopsided. On one side stand the three hundred confident and colorful Baal priests. The authority of Ahab and Jezebel backs them up. And there stands the *Troubler*—alone and physically unimpressive. You might think the contrast would be intimidating enough to send him packing.

The *Troubler* explains the consequences. Yahweh will either prove that what the *Troubler* has been preaching is true, or he will have to retire from the field in defeat. He must then be willing to share deity with Baal. Defeat will force him to accept the limited responsibility and power assigned to him.

But if Yahweh vindicates the *Troubler*'s message, all of Baal's claims will go up in smoke. His lie will be forever exposed.

"You go first," the *Troubler* gestures to the Baal priests. They are ready; they have arranged a bull on Baal's altar and are organized for prayer.

All morning long they implore Baal to consume the sacrifice. With charged expectation, we wait. Baal will not fail. Fire will fall.

But *nothing* happens. Children complain. They have drunk the precious supply of water their mothers brought. Exposed to the blazing sun, some people faint. We are puzzled. Why is Baal silent?

Since late morning the *Troubler* has been taunting the priests. As their prayers became more feverish, his mockery accelerated. "Maybe your god went off somewhere to think. Perhaps he went down the hill to use the bathroom. Maybe Baal is on a journey. Maybe he is out of earshot. Yell louder. He might be asleep!"

The mockery continues. But Baal is as silent as a tomb.

In the crowd we turn to each other and ask, "Why does Baal tolerate such insults?"

Panic shows on the faces of the Baal priests.

We are horrified. In desperation the priests begin to lacerate themselves. Blood gushes out, covering their clothes, hands, and faces. The spectacle causes children to turn their faces. Women wail. Some men vomit!

Baal is still silent. No fire falls.

In midafternoon, Elijah commands the exhausted priests to "shut up and get out of the way!"

The priests retire in defeat and humiliation.

Elijah calls to my neighbors and me. I feel as though his eyes are fixed *on me*. "How long do you intend to continue your divided loyalties? You are hopping along like birds, trying to put one foot on a Baal branch and one on a Yahweh branch."

Now Elijah is preparing the altar of Yahweh. We watch in disbelief. First he digs a trench around the altar. Then he arranges the wood. Next he lifts big slabs of raw meat and arranges them on the altar. The smell of bloody flesh drifts over me.

He tells men to pour water on the sacrifice. "More!" "More water!" he yells. Three times Elijah soaks the sacrifice. Water runs down, filling the trench. How did he get that water?

No one can believe what we are seeing. "That fool!" I hear myself yelling. "He has blown all chances for success."

While we are murmuring, Elijah wipes his hands on his hairy coat, backs away, kneels, and begins to pray. "O Lord, you are God. Answer so that these sinful people may know that you alone are God. Turn their divided hearts to you."

No sooner are the words out of Elijah's mouth than Yahweh answers. Long sheets of fire crackle from the sky. Everyone jumps back, dumbstruck by fear. The fire licks up the sacrifice, wood, stones, and water—all in one holy and awesome gulp. Whoosh! Only ashes, a few pieces of charred wood, and scorched earth remain.

Holy terror fills the air. Some people are crying like babies—including strong men. Some have fallen on their faces. Others have dropped to their knees—heads bowed and covered. Children have been shocked into stunned silence.

Suddenly, I comprehend why Elijah called us to Mount Carmel. I am shocked by Baal's absolute silence. Now I see those priests in their fancy robes for what they really are: crafty deceivers. All their boasts and claims are lies, and we have been their stooges. There is no God but Yahweh! All who believe otherwise are fools. He can't be confined to a corner and made to share his deity with others. We the people of Israel must own up to our idolatrous ways, all our divided loyalties. Yahweh is Lord of all, the giver of life, and the source of everything good.

With one voice my kinsmen and I cry out, "Yahweh alone is our God. There is no God but the Lord! He is the Lord of all things! Away with Baal!"

Then Elijah tells us urgently, "Go home. It's going to rain!" That's good news for a man whose name—"Jubal"—means "stream" or "creek."

As I left the mountain, I picked up a piece of charred wood. It has become a memorial for my family and me to what happened there that day.

Getting Ready to Hear
(Chapter 2)

When judged by economic, military, and political standards, the reign of Jeroboam II (786-746 BC) was the most successful of all the kings of Israel. When judged by fidelity to the Mosaic Covenant, his reign marked one of Israel's lowest points. Among the failures was the belief that faithfulness to God could be satisfied through lavish support for the sanctuaries at Dan and Bethel. People meticulously went through the motions of worship, but their hearts were elsewhere.

Into this scene stepped a lay preacher from Judah whose name was Amos, one of the twelve minor prophets. He pronounced God's judgment upon "mechanical piety" that expects God to be satisfied just because the habitual pieces of worship are in place. He knew that when worship becomes routine—manageable and lifeless—we cease to commune with God, and he with us. No longer is the Holy God free to judge and transform his people. He becomes incidental. The Conspiracy succeeds; the worshipper is in charge.

The Baal of mechanical piety has plagued God's people from the start. A few decades after Amos ministered in the North, Isaiah confronted the same problem in Judah (Isa. 1:10-20).

Amos's chief opponent was Amaziah—official priest of the Bethel sanctuary. In this chapter, Amaziah tells the story of Amos's assault on the Baal of mechanical piety.

The pertinent scriptures are 2 Kings 14:23-29 and the Book of Amos. Amaziah appears in 7:10-17. For a summary of true worship read Isa. 58.

— 2 —

THE BAAL OF MECHANICAL PIETY

Maybe you have heard of me. My name is Amaziah. I began humbly, but quickly learned the rules for climbing up. By "playing the game" I became the official priest of the royal sanctuary at Bethel in Israel—the so-called Northern Kingdom. I delighted in the many religious, civic, and political privileges that came with my position. Social elites thought no party complete unless I was there to crown it with my good humor and aura of importance. I rode the crest of a favorable religious tide among the populace. Israel's priests were well funded, and the two royal sanctuaries where Yahweh was worshipped were well attended. Perhaps best of all, I enjoyed a cozy relationship with King Jeroboam II. My problems were happy ones.

Of course, there were nuisances from time to time. One day one of my assistants mentioned in passing that a rough-looking man from Judah had wandered across the border and started preaching in Gilgal. I had other things to think about that day and didn't pay much attention. I thought, "Let the zealot vent his frustrations over our successes, and then we will herd him south again."

EVERYTHING WAS COMING UP ROSY

What a grand time to have been alive and enjoy my perks as an official priest. Those were golden years for Israel and me. Whether you considered politics, military success, economics, or religion, all sectors of society were booming (except for the class of social failures who littered our beautiful landscape).

Jeroboam II had been king about thirty-five years when I first received word of the southern preacher. Jeroboam's remarkable accomplishments demonstrated his agility as an administrator. All of us had reason to think that history would honor him as one of Israel's most capable kings. He embodied our national pride.

Never before had a king of Israel ruled unchallenged over so much territory. During Jeroboam's reign Israel had the good fortune of a weakened Syria. The king even captured parts of it, including Damascus its capital. Assyria was far away, nursing wounds it suffered from a failed attack on Syria. Jeroboam defeated the king of Moab. All the territory once lost to Israel's enemies was recovered. No expense was spared to create impressive fortifications.

At first, Jeroboam treated the Southern Kingdom harshly, as Joash his father had done. However, he later realized that friendship and mutual support were more beneficial. The two kingdoms came to control all the territory once ruled by Solomon.

Had you been there, you would have been impressed by our cultural achievements and material prosperity. They were especially apparent in Samaria, our capital. The wealthy lived in unprecedented luxury. For starters, one could point to their opulent summer and winter homes. They were customarily appointed with imported ivories. Oh, what gala events I enjoyed there.

The mercantile economy of nearby Phoenicia was flourishing, and Israel was collecting its share of profits from trade between the two countries. Jeroboam's conquests in Transjordan placed him in control of the trade routes leading from Syria, and the commercial highways that came from Arabia. He collected tariffs from both sources. Israel profited from selling olive oil and wine to Egypt and Assyria. Starting with the royal court and the merchant class, well-positioned people were reaping the benefits. The marketplaces were crowded with people and bountifully stocked with imported wares.

No one could remember a time of such national wealth and military security.

BEST OF ALL

However, as an official priest, I was even more pleased with Israel's religious successes. The royal sanctuaries at Bethel in the South and Dan in the North were in pristine condition. The other priests attached to the sanctuaries were well trained and well paid. They were comfortably integrated into the social structure. So, in addition to their priestly functions, the priests were expected by everyone to grace civic and cultural activities with their presence. You might say they knew how to "grease a social event."

As priests, we were careful to nurture the Mosaic tradition by observing the great sacrificial ceremonies, feasts, and fasts. We conducted covenant-renewal ceremonies that resembled the one Joshua conducted at Shechem. The Levites—who, as a group, assisted priests in the temple—were active in the villages. They taught the great convictions of Israel's faith. As part of our religious heritage, we even possessed a document that told the history of the Mosaic Covenant from our country's perspective.

I could confidently report that the state of religion in Israel was commendable. Sacrifices were offered each morning. Tithes were presented every third day. Freewill offerings came regularly. All of this happened in an atmosphere of impressive ritual.

Who could have blamed me for thinking that Israel's enviable role on the stage of history would only improve? That is, as soon as that troublesome southern preacher could be sent packing.

THE INTRUDER

My initial inattention to the *Intruder* was a mistake. He didn't go home, and he didn't shut up. Reports reached me that his words were beginning to create a nuisance. People were not accustomed to preachers shouting their messages in public. They expected religious spokesmen to be cultured, more urbane. A few days after the initial report, I sent two assistants to hear the zealot and bring a report. I began to build a case against him, just in case I needed to inform the king. It seemed appropriate to call him the *Intruder*. The bottom line was that he must go home.

A few days later, the two assistants returned and made their report. What I heard angered me and all those around me.

At first, the people who had paused to listen to the *Intruder* complimented his message. He claimed that Yahweh had sent him into Israel. He had been busy doing other things when Yahweh irresistibly commissioned him to declare his word in the North. Of course, that provoked laughter in the crowd. With that absurdity forgiven, the crowd listened. He proclaimed that God was about to judge the small nations surrounding Israel. Cheers went up. Anything God wanted to do to punish Israel's neighbors would meet with our approval. Everyone could think of some reason the surrounding countries should be punished.

But all of a sudden the *Intruder* shifted his focus, and the crowd's mood darkened. He began to say that the fire of God's judgment would fall upon Israel also. He pushed absurdity to the extreme by saying God would use Assyria as his instrument of judgment. His words so contradicted Israel's peaceful and prosperous climate that my agents immediately dismissed him as a religious nut—too much southern sun on the brain. Their assessment was fortified when the *Intruder* described how the Assyrian sword would fall. Cities would be destroyed. Political collapse would occur, and citizens would be marched into exile.

What nonsense. The very notion that God would direct his wrath against his own people!

Wait. More was to come.

The *Intruder* told his listeners he had nothing new to say. He was just restating the conditions for giving exclusive loyalty to Yahweh. Those conditions had been made clear in the Mosaic Covenant. He rehearsed the events in which God had revealed himself. Beginning with the Exodus, the *Intruder* moved forward. He named the great convictions—now ignored—that had distinguished God's people from the surrounding nations. Yahweh had bound himself to the covenant relationship. He would be the God of Israel, and Israel would serve him in undivided love.

With that, the *Intruder* concluded his condemnation and retired from the scene. The crowd and my assistants hoped they had seen the last of him. People asked each other, "What prompted that explosion?"

A couple of days after receiving the first report, news reached me that the *Intruder* had not returned home. He had popped up in Rimmon. I dispatched three more assistants to report on his activity. A few days later, they returned and conveyed their shock and disbelief. By then, it wasn't difficult for the *Intruder* to draw a crowd. The three agents reported that as the people gathered around, the *Intruder* asked them a question. "Are you puzzled over why the judgment of God will fall upon Israel?"

Of course the people were puzzled. The question had been bouncing around since the first outburst.

The *Intruder* proceeded to answer his own question. The crowd's anger boiled.

He charged that the people of Israel—including priests and prophets—had completely misunderstood God's special calling to the Exodus people. Israel had concluded that because it had a special calling from God, it also had his guarantee for political and material success, victory and prestige among the nations. True, our covenant renewal ceremonies carefully reaffirmed God's promise of material and national blessing.

The *Intruder* continued. The Exodus people—including Judah—had been known by God as had no others. They could not plead ignorance of his ways. Nevertheless, Israel had failed to see that along with election came increased responsibility. It had heard only the promise of increased political and material benefits. Perhaps most deadly, Israel had failed to see that apart from covenantal faithfulness, election meant nothing. The *Intruder* even said that lacking such faithfulness, God valued Israel no more than he did the Ethiopians.

By this time, the crowd was aghast. Then things got worse. The *Intruder* said that Yahweh is the God of all nations, all peoples. He had brought other nations to their national homelands, even though they did not know it. God's sovereignty embraces all people.

This homespun preacher had positively lost his mind. Maybe that explained why he wandered north.

One of the most cherished features of our religious expectations was the coming day of the Lord. It would be a time when God's blessings upon us would exceed anything he had bestowed in the past. We could only imagine its splendor.

Insanely, the *Intruder* contradicted everything we expected. He said the day of the Lord—as we imagined it—only demonstrated our spiritual blindness. It showed how little we knew about the ways of Yahweh.

The great day of the Lord, the *Intruder* proclaimed, would be a time of darkness, not light; judgment, not promise; destruction, not building. "Why," he cried, "do you want the day of the Lord to come? It will be like a person fleeing from a lion, only to be attacked by a bear."

Understandably, the *Intruder*'s impudence scandalized his listeners. Surely something had disconnected his tongue from his mind.

Then the preacher seemed to lose control completely. He said Israel was like a ripe crop about to be consumed by locusts. It was like the waters of the earth about to be licked up by supernatural fire. It was like a wall shown to be crooked by using a plumb line. Israel was like a basket of rotting summer fruit. He even sang a funeral dirge over us.

By then the crowd had heard enough. In anger bordering on outright violence they shouted the *Intruder* into silence. Silenced, but unbowed, he retreated.

THE CONFRONTATION

By then, I knew the *Intruder* would not leave by himself. I would have to force him out. I had concluded that his destination was the shrine at Bethel—symbol of our religious accomplishments. That would be intolerable. I sent word to the king, telling him the *Intruder* was conspiring against him. He was generating social unrest by telling the people they would go into exile.

I had predicted correctly. Two days later the *Intruder* showed up at Bethel and began another of his senseless sermons. Emotionally unhinged, he babbled something about God condemning our Bethel altar. I watched and listened from the shadows. As his tirade accelerated, I knew a confrontation was inevitable.

Had you been with me, you would have noticed his mood darkening and his pace increasing. Absurdly, he accused our healthy nation of being deathly ill—a self-inflicted illness no less. The disease, he charged, was a sickness of soul, a deadly cancer. What we called vigorous health, God called stinking, decaying flesh.

"Do you want to know the details of how wretched your 'piety' really is? I will tell you."

He began by indicting the unchecked greed hiding beneath the fashionable skirts of our flourishing economy. Our temple worship and professed faithfulness to Yahweh did not translate into justice executed on behalf of the defenseless. The *Intruder* accused us of oppressing the poor and crushing the needy. He challenged, "In the Exodus, did God not bind all Israel together as a mutually caring family?"

Accusations flew. Our wealthy merchants habitually lusted for economic power. Flaunting their insider influence, they trampled on the heads of the poor. Our leaders, corrupted by opulence, exhibited their luxury by lying on beds of ease. They showed no sorrow for having prostituted the covenant.

Absent of cultural refinement, the *Intruder* compared our fashionable women to the fat, sleek cows of Bashan. Morally vacuous social butterflies, they were urging their husbands on to even more rapacious behavior.

Had you been standing nearby, you would have heard the *Intruder* training his accusations on our legal system—charging that it had become corrupt. Through bribery, our courts had become but one more way to fatten the greed of the commercial class and to refuse fundamental justice to the oppressed. All of this, he charged, demonstrated that although we honored God with our lips, our hearts were far from him.

Then the *Intruder* paused and fixed his heated gaze on *me*. He waited until all eyes were on *me*. Then he unleashed his ultimate indictment like a hunter releasing a falcon. He charged that the entire religious establishment had defaulted on its primary responsibility to Yahweh and the covenant. "With you, Amaziah, as one of the most influential defectors, the religious establishment has abetted the lusts of a corrupt culture. You have spoken not one word of judgment against the injustices and exploitations going on in the shadows of your places of worship."

That, the *Intruder* intoned, was the terminal sickness destroying Israel. It exposed a deep estrangement from Yahweh. It confirmed that Israel had, in spite of its impressive religious apparatus, corrupted its covenant calling. In language I strongly resented, the *Intruder* said God desires repentance, is anxious to forgive, and longs for authentic reconciliation with Israel.

How foolish, I thought. What was there to forgive?

Then he simply "broke the camel's back." The priests and I had regularly told the people that when our elaborate sacrificial structure was correctly administered, God was satisfied. What God wanted most, we had eloquently delivered. But the *Intruder* insisted that God was neither impressed nor satisfied—not in the least. He reminded us that during Israel's forty years of wilderness sojourn, the Exodus people brought no sacrifices to Yahweh, yet they worshipped him in truth.

The point of no return had been exceeded. I could no longer restrain my fury.

Before I could interrupt, the *Intruder* unloaded one final outburst. He told us that God hated and despised our entire religious scene—all our feasts and solemn assemblies. Claiming to speak for Yahweh, he cried out, "I am sick of your loud but hollow songs. Take them away, and remove your melodious harps as well." The *Intruder* asked, "So what does God want from you?" He claimed to answer for God: "Let justice pour across the land like a flood, and let righteousness flow like an unending stream."

Livid with anger, I stepped forward. It was time to silence this impudent farce.

"Amos," I thundered, "Israel cannot tolerate your words. Flee to the land of Judah. If you want to prophesy, then do it there. Never again come to Bethel. This is the sanctuary of the king, a temple of the kingdom. Go home! We have enough prophets of our own."

In what I took to be a surly reply, the *Intruder* said the whole of Israel was hopelessly blind. Consequently, God's judgment would fall upon us—the Assyrians would destroy Israel. He even said that I would die in an unclean land but not before my wife had been made a harlot, my sons and daughters had perished by the sword, and the conqueror had seized my prized land.

With that, he was done. He returned home. I never saw him again.

MY NAME REVIVED?

Approximately four years after the confrontation, Jeroboam II died. Then catastrophe struck. Just as Amos had warned, the

Assyrians, whom we had ignored, began to stir. Shortly after Jeroboam's death, Tiglath-pileser III seized the Assyrian throne. He created a military machine such as the world had never witnessed. He conquered Babylonia and then turned his attention westward.

You will not be surprised to learn that I was seized by terror when I received news of his coming. Every informed citizen knew that neither Syria nor Israel could stand. Within a brief twenty-four-year period after Jeroboam's death, our beloved Israel would succumb to the Assyrian onslaught. As Amos had warned, our feasts would look like funerals, and our happy songs would turn to sorrow.

In the meantime, Israel began to collapse internally. After Jeroboam's death, six kings reigned amid political and social deterioration. The last one, Hoshea, died in Assyrian chains.

The Assyrians introduced a military policy never before seen. It was designed to break the spirit of conquered peoples. They moved most of the people out of Israel and forced them to settle in parts of the Assyrian Empire. I was one of them. The Assyrians moved other conquered people into Israel. The disruption was devastating. It inflicted a wound from which I will never recover.

My battle with the southern preacher happened more than thirty years ago. The day is still fresh on my mind. And so are the horrible events that followed. I am now a withered old man. Almost no one who lives near my Assyrian hovel shares my memories and grief. I often wonder, "Is Amos still alive?"

"Amaziah"—"Jehovah is my strength"—is my name. Nothing about me bears witness to my name. Broken, I am but a shadow of my former arrogant self. But in my brokenness, in my exile, the God of Amos has graciously found me. He has repeated the prophet's words I once scorned: "Israel, you can still return to me. You can seek me and live."

Now, I have big decisions to make. What will I do with my memories? What will I do with my name? How will I respond to Jehovah?

Getting Ready to Hear

(Chapter 3)

Sometime during the reign of Ahaz, king of Judah (735-715 BC), a rural prophet named Micah came to Jerusalem. He lacked the credentials of city-bred prophets, but God had commissioned him to prophesy to Israel and Judah. He spoke on behalf of poor farmers who were suffering at the hands of powerful landlords. Micah believed the cancerous corruption of Israel had spread into Judah. His critique wasn't due to any failure by Judah to maintain the forms of worship. Outwardly, the worship of Yahweh was elaborate, expensive, and impressive. The problem was that people thought God could be manipulated through their worship. Worship had descended into magic—just a tool in the worshippers' hands used to put God in an agreeable and rewarding frame of mind. That was the guise the Conspiracy had assumed. In that regard, it was identical to the way surrounding pagan cultures "worshipped" their deities. Micah proclaimed that such treatment of Yahweh amounts to apostasy. A "god" who can be controlled by what we say and do in "worship" isn't Yahweh.

The commandment not to take the name of the Lord in vain (Exod. 20:7) is a warning against using God's name for contrived human purposes. Scholars tell us that Israel always faced the danger of using the divine Name (Yahweh) to keep God under their (magical) control. The God of the covenant is the Lord, not the servant of the people. This danger never passes.

One of the most riveting parts of the Book of Micah is cast in the form of a covenant lawsuit in which one party to a covenant charges the other with breech of contract. In this instance, Yahweh is the aggrieved party. Israel and Judah are hauled into court to hear Yahweh's charges. A verdict is rendered.

The book's covenant lawsuit is the setting for this chapter. One of the royal judges indicted by God tells the story. Although there were royal judges in Jerusalem, "Eliakim" is fictional.

The pertinent scripture is the Book of Micah, especially 1:2-9; 6:1-8.

— 3 —

WORSHIP OR MANIPULATION?

I am Eliakim—a proud member of the royal family of Judah. The king assigned me to be one of the royal judges in Jerusalem. My royalty and judicial responsibilities bring immense social influence. Until the time of King Jehoshaphat, only elders were judges. Elders still are in smaller communities.

Court is held in one of the designated chambers on each side of a city gate's open space. Sessions occur each Monday and Thursday, but never during festivals. Court recesses during Nisan when barley is harvested and Tishri when grapes are harvested. We never begin a court session in the afternoon lest it interfere with afternoon prayers.

The first document the court issues after a plaintiff lodges a complaint is a "summons" to the defendant. It fixes the trial date and is delivered by a "messenger of the court." On court days a colorful cross section of the city streams in. Tension and noise mount outside. In the summer the courtroom is hot and smelly. In any court session, royal judges might rule on the cases of orphans and widows, scholars and shop owners, traders and landowners.

Today, *apprehension* plagues me. I am also livid with *anger.* Conflict between the two emotions has temporarily knocked me off balance. Normally, I project a public image of self-control and self-confidence befitting my royalty. I use this to intimidate litigants and accent my influence.

THE SUMMONS

I am accustomed to signing summonses and sending court messengers to defendants. Because I am royalty, no messenger of the court has ever come to me. That has changed. A summons has been delivered to all the royal judges. We have been indicted and named as codefendants. The list of defendants includes the religious, political, and civic leaders of Israel. The kings of Israel and Judah are included. Even average citizens are named.

Just receiving a summons would be shocking enough. Even more jolting is the plaintiff's identity: *Yahweh himself*—the God of Abraham and Moses. The Creator of heaven and earth is hauling us into court. He will come from his heavenly temple to press his case against us. That is the reason for my fear.

Yahweh's accusation is extremely startling. He has lodged a covenant lawsuit against Israel and Judah. We are being charged with apostasy—defection from the terms of the covenant. The summons accuses that, without admitting it, we have abandoned pure worship of Yahweh. He has been faithful in his love for us, but we have not reciprocated.

Yahweh's court messenger has not been discreet. He has announced Yahweh's summons in the city's public spaces. Priests and the temple bureaucracy have heard it. Merchants, bankers, and traders have been verbally accosted. Shock and disbelief have seized the city. Almost everyone thinks that the summons is unjustified and that the messenger is insane.

After the initial trauma receded a bit, I regained some of my royal composure. As a veteran jurist, I began to formulate a defense. Rather quickly, I was able to check off a battery of witnesses who could verify my peoples' innocence. The elaborate temple rituals and festivals we so lavishly support will be a good place to start.

Out of legal habit, I wondered, "If the judges are included as defendants, who will pronounce the verdict in Yahweh's cause? Will he have a spokesman as permitted? Where will the pleadings be heard?" Normally when several persons are charged, one plaintiff is permitted to speak for all. "Who will speak for Israel and Judah?"

Yahweh himself has fixed the date. The proceedings will be intense. But the evidence is clearly on our side.

THE COURT MESSENGER

Yahweh has chosen an unsavory person from the social margins to be his messenger of the court. He is a farmer who hails from Moresheth-gath—a village twenty-two miles southeast of Jerusalem. He is the reason for my anger. Rather than being a refined and respectable city dweller, the farmer is a rustic—better suited for barns and fields than courts. An offensive odor hangs on his rough clothes. Repulsive stains cover his boots.

I recoil at everything about this man, for I am accustomed to having people address me as their social superior or as a royal peer. Social subordinates habitually show deference. Woe to them if they do not. But this farmer is void of deference. Arrogance seems to be more his style. He goes around the city issuing his indictment and summons and declaring that he is "filled with the spirit of the Lord and a love for justice." He says God's power motivates him. Judah and Israel, he preaches, have defaulted from the covenant, and Yahweh has appointed him to announce the charges.

Actually, I find the farmer's boldness quite unsettling. If I encounter him again, I will treat him to a royal lesson in subservience.

THE TRIAL

The dreaded trial date arrives. Defendants assemble. Awe dominates.

Yahweh has arrived. The Holy God's coming was as though he were walking upon the high places of the earth. It was as though valleys were splitting before him, and mountains were melting beneath his feet. Holy terror has shaken my self-confidence.

In this trial, Yahweh will be the prosecutor and presiding judge. He also will pronounce the concluding judgment.

Yahweh has chosen a spokesman, and I am horrified by his choice. *It's that farmer!* He is void of credentials. I think of inserting an objection—but remain silent.

Yahweh names and seats his chosen judges. They are strange indeed. He has summoned the nations of the earth. He has even called forth the earth's foundations and its lofty mountains.

THE CHARGES

Speaking through the farmer, Yahweh begins to present his case against Israel and Judah—against me.

First, he gives both countries opportunity to speak. He asks all of us to show what he has done to make us weary of being his covenantal partners. What has he done to provoke our compromised loyalty?

Opportunity to respond comes and passes without my raising an objection. Yahweh's record of faithfulness is impeccable.

Yahweh says we have forgotten what it means to be his people. He recounts the history of his care for us. It was he who delivered us from Egyptian slavery. He sent Moses, Aaron, and Miriam to be our instruments of freedom. He defended us against our enemies during our perilous journey to Canaan.

Have we forgotten the many acts of redemption executed on our behalf? Have we forgotten God's steadfast love?

Yahweh formally begins to present his case. He says that our cities, especially Samaria and Jerusalem, have become engines of corruption. He has observed Israel's and Judah's failure to connect worship with love for the neighbor. In our commercial and private, religious and legal affairs, we act as though the neighbor—especially the defenseless—can just be omitted from the covenant. Showing mercy and doing justice have fallen by the wayside.

Yahweh says he has been watching the powerful. What he has seen justifies his accusations. He has observed our religious zeal and lavish temple ceremonies. The three daily prayers we enthusiastically offer have not gone unnoticed. But Yahweh has also seen how we lie awake at night, devising wickedness we can inflict on others. Zealous worship hasn't kept judges and others in places of influence from taking bribes. For money, Yahweh charges, we are willing to rip the skin from the backs of defenseless people.

Despite our religious zeal, Yahweh insists, we hate the good and love the evil. Wealthy landowners in both countries—in league with corrupt judges and bankers—exploit poor farmers. Because of excessive interest rates and taxes, many small farmers lose their ancestral lands. Taxes suck up whatever surpluses poor farmers produce. Dishonest scales are in the employ of many merchants. In general, Yahweh concludes, a very low moral tone characterizes Israel and Judah.

Much of the blame, he says, should be placed on civil and religious leaders in both countries. They have acted as though it is possible to please God while scheming to abuse power. Religious, commercial, and political institutions have failed to promote covenantal faithfulness and moral integrity. Instead, they regularly conspire to inflate greed and exploit the needy.

Of course, Yahweh hasn't overlooked how lavishly Judah and Israel underwrite the mechanics of the covenant. But both countries have worked equally hard to make their worship a party to their infidelity. They have bought off the prophets and extracted sham messages of peace and divine approval. The prophets, like our priests whose teachings can be dictated by money, have abandoned Yahweh's mandate to speak truth to power. As a group, they have led God's people astray.

"Why," Yahweh asks us, "do you boast of your religious zeal, when your lives contradict my character?"

While we are reeling from the impact of Yahweh's charge, he moves on to intensify the indictment. He says that in the temple we make a great show of taking him seriously. But Judah's impressive temple apparatus, and Israel's shrines at Dan and Bethel, would convince only the religiously superficial that we truly know God.

The blessings Yahweh has showered upon us have not prompted pure worship. Instead, they have amplified our greed. Our rampant envy reveals that we don't know and trust him.

Then Yahweh cuts to the marrow of his charges. He says that our zealous but superficial worship springs from a fundamental misrepresentation of who he is. We have not worshipped him exclusively. Instead, we have treated him like a pagan deity. Rather than lovingly entrusting ourselves to him—letting him be God on his own terms—our "worship" is just a chance to manipulate him—just as we manipulate Baal. This is the real purpose of our costly gifts and impressive rituals.

Yahweh is not at all swayed by our lavish offerings and sacrifices. He tells us that even if we were to offer him a thousand rams and ten thousand rivers of olive oil, we would not have touched his heart.

THE JUDGMENT

Acting as the presiding judge, Yahweh now pronounces his judgment.

Israel and Judah are guilty of turning away from Yahweh, even while boasting of their fidelity. The nations and earth's foundations concur.

We have behaved as though Yahweh can be controlled by magic. The whole temple culture, Yahweh says with disgust, has become a tool for our scheme. "Is there any wonder," he asks, "why systematic corruption has overtaken your two countries?"

YAHWEH'S QUESTION AND ANSWER

Yahweh pauses, fixes his gaze upon us, and asks, "What offerings do I expect from you? What do I require of my covenant people?"

He answers: "I want you to practice justice, show my kind of love to others, and walk before me in genuine humility."

Not in slaughtered rams is true worship expressed but in all of human life being conformed—in obedient love—to the gracious God who practices justice and shows his love to others.

OUR RESPONSE?

Yahweh and his judges have withdrawn. Finally, I gain strength to speak. But instead of offering a bold defense, I raise more questions. "That's it? That's 'all' God requires? *Practice justice, show his love to others, and walk humbly before him?* No crafty maneuvering to collect divine rewards? Meeting God in the person of my neighbor? Who has ever heard of a God like that?"

Silence!

Here comes Micah the farmer. He has a hopeful look on his face.

Getting Ready to Hear

(Chapter 4)

Never does the Prince of Darkness act more craftily, or succeed more effectively, than when he deceives God's people into worshipping what were meant to be instruments for manifesting God's holiness and love. Instruments might be Christian ministers, religious symbols, church buildings, one's education, or even Christian denominations. The transition from instrument to idol is subtle and deadly. Usually, we don't see it coming.

This chapter traces one of the error's clearest occurrences found in Scripture. Part of the story happened shortly after the king of Arad blocked Israel's entrance into Canaan. Another part occurred during the reign of Hezekiah, king of Judah (ca. 715—687 BC). The event around which this chapter revolves occurred before Sennacherib, king of Assyria, invaded Judah during the fourteenth year of Hezekiah's reign.

The pertinent scriptures are Num. 21:1-9 and 2 Kings 18:1-8.

— 4 —

HOW TO TREAT A SNAKE

As an influential businessman in Jerusalem, I have mixed evaluations of Hezekiah—our young king. Most of my business associates and social contacts share my opinions.

But now he has gone overboard and must be stopped. He has taken marginally acceptable religious reform one step too far. Unrest among the populace is cresting and could become violent if the king carries out his most recent aim.

Given my commercial and social connections, I am well positioned to take the city's pulse. The king's anticipated action has sparked sharp protests among some members of the priesthood. Grumblings can be heard among members of the military and the bureaucracy. The marketplace and industrial zones of the city are all abuzz with simmering unrest.

I should inform you that in recent years, my pottery manufacturing business has experienced robust growth. I own manufacturing facilities in eight nearby villages. Managers of those factories have told me of growing unrest in the countryside over the king's recently announced target of religious renewal. The last thing I need is unchecked religious zeal that disrupts my business.

NOT HIS FATHER'S SON

The new king's father, Ahaz, was a disaster. To save his own political hide, he was willing to make Judah a vassal of Assyria. Erosion of the worship of Yahweh is largely attributable to him.

My business and many others suffered because of the special taxes Ahaz levied and then shipped off to Nineveh as tribute. In public, my friends and I always bowed and scraped before him. Privately, we held him in contempt. We were shamed by the dishonor Assyria heaped on us.

Ahaz seemed to have an unlimited capacity for absorbing Assyria's insults. I recall how the prophet Isaiah desperately urged Ahaz to resist Assyria and trust God's promises—all to no avail.

Ahaz's name meant "Whom Yahweh holds fast." It should have been "Whom Assyria holds fast."

Our collective economic necks were rubbed raw by the Assyrian yoke. But more galling than that, Ahaz installed an altar to Ashur in the Jerusalem temple. Ashur is chief god of the Assyrian pantheon. This amounted to converting much of the temple into a pagan shrine. Yes, I know that as a vassal, Ahaz had to acknowledge Assyria's gods as his own. But that did not lessen our shame.

Until now, King Hezekiah has given us reason to be proud. He seems to have learned from his father's errors. He is a wise and vigorous leader. Hezekiah has removed the Assyrian altar from the temple, an act Assyria will see as rebellion. Hezekiah is beginning to resist Assyrian demands, intends to refuse paying tribute, and is strengthening the military. He has already recaptured some of the cities his father surrendered to the Philistines.

Many of us think Hezekiah will get away with his nationalistic strategy for only a short time. We know the Assyrian king's attention is momentarily focused on fighting his enemies close to home. So Hezekiah's rebellion is laced with considerable risks.

As a keen observer of international politics, Hezekiah knows a conspiracy against Assyria is building. Several Philistine city-states have refused to pay tribute. Egypt is fanning the fires. There is reason to believe that before long, the Assyrian province of Babylonia will add fuel to the rebellion. Hezekiah is tempted to join—even help lead—the revolution.

He knows that international unrest could eventually bring the Assyrian war machine into Judah. If that happens, Assyria will strike, and strike hard, ravaging the countryside and besieging Jerusalem. Looking ahead, Hezekiah and his engineers are preparing for all possibilities. He is demonstrating considerable foresight by strengthening the city's walls.

Another of his projects is simply astonishing. If the Assyrian army were to lay siege to Jerusalem, the city would soon run out of fresh water. Most of our water comes from a conduit that runs from the Spring of Gihon, located outside the city. The Assyrians could easily disrupt the source and force the city to surrender. The brutal consequences would be unspeakable. But Hezekiah has a plan.

I have learned from my engineer son-in-law that Hezekiah intends to dig what he will call the Siloam Tunnel. It will run seventeen hundred feet through solid rock. The tunnel will tap the Spring of Gihon and bring water to the Pool of Siloam inside the city. Workers equipped with wedges, hammers, and picks will dig the tunnel.

Even more astonishing, instead of digging from one direction and eating up precious time, the workers will bore from both ends of the tunnel. If all goes well, they will meet in the middle. The city will be assured of fresh water, no matter what the Assyrians do.

Standing up to Assyria has inspired a wave of patriotism. But satisfaction over Hezekiah's stiff resistance is only part of the story. Some of his actions have generated resentment throughout Judah.

WHY DISRUPT A SUCCESSFUL ARRANGEMENT?

Not only has Hezekiah proved to be a staunch patriot, but he is something of a religious fanatic also. And therein lies the problem.

At the beginning of his reign, Hezekiah began to repair the neglected temple. He reorganized the services of the priests and Levites. Then he reopened the temple with impressive sacrifices, musical instruments, and singing. He had sent invitations throughout Judah and even to Israel. His letter of invitation began, "O people of Israel, return to the Lord." The Passover was celebrated. It was marked by more rejoicing than had occurred since the days of Solomon. For seven days, our people sang and praised the Lord.

All of that was acceptable. But it was part of a much larger and more alarming project.

Most of us have become accustomed to religious accommodations that make it possible to worship Yahweh in the temple, and Baal and his lovers in shrines outside Jerusalem. Most folk, including many of the temple priests, are comfortable with this long-standing arrangement.

But not Hezekiah. And not the prophets Isaiah and Micah.

Hezekiah has unleashed sweeping religious reforms such as have not been seen since the time of David. He intends to purge Judah of Baal worship, while also attacking social injustices he says undercut the worship of Yahweh. Hezekiah constantly reminds us of how Baal worship corrupted Israel to the North and brought down God's judgment by the Assyrians. He intends to restore Jerusalem as the center where the Holy One alone is worshipped. Faithful service to Yahweh in all things must be revived.

Hezekiah intends to rip out Baal worship by its roots. He has already terminated the offerings of first fruits from the earth and the first born of cattle to Baal. Baal altars, Asherah poles, and sacred pillars are being burned or torn down. Baal shrines are being destroyed. All sacred objects used to worship Baal must be destroyed.

His cry is, "Purify, Purify!"

Hezekiah's zeal is meeting with considerable resentment. I share the resentment. Why upset an arrangement that has worked so well? Haven't we given Yahweh his due? The king should have gradually introduced his reforms. People need time to adjust before they abandon their old ways. "Don't jerk the rudder."

EXTREME RELIGION

As I have mentioned, even worse is on the way. Hezekiah is about to tamper with something we prize highly. He intends to disrupt our sacred past, to destroy something essential for our worship of Yahweh.

Permit me to explain. Centuries ago, when our ancestors were journeying from Egypt to Canaan, they had a bad habit of complaining against the Lord. The journey had been very long. There had already been battles with the Canaanites. Our ancestors were beginning another long trek—this time from Mount Hor south toward the Red Sea. Discouraged and frustrated, their impatience boiled over in complaints against God and Moses. "You are a sorry leader, Moses, bringing us into this wilderness to die! We are thirsting to death. Food is almost impossible to find. And we are sick of this nasty manna."

By then, God had taken all the junk he could from our contentious fathers. He unleashed fiery serpents upon them; many people died. In panic, they cried out to Moses for help. They confessed their sin and asked Moses to petition God for relief. God instructed Moses to "make a bronze serpent, and place it on a pole." All who were bitten were supposed to look at the bronze serpent. In looking, they would live.

Through the centuries our religious leaders have preserved the pole and the bronze serpent. The serpent occupies an important place in the temple; it is a fixture of our faith. The serpent is an irreplaceable reminder of God's presence and guidance, a sure sign of his salvation.

Now, Hezekiah is speaking like a religious fanatic. As absurd as it might sound, he wants to destroy the bronze serpent and the pole. A date has been set.

The news has spread like wildfire. The reaction has been predictable: "Our king has gone mad!"

On the morning of the appointed day, I stand in front of my shop—rows of pottery for sale displayed behind me—and watch a colorful and noisy cross section of Judean society stream by. Shepherds, farmers, shopkeepers from the villages, and tradesmen who ply the caravan routes stride into view and move on. Many of the men have brought their wives, children, and slaves. Soldiers and members of the king's court pass by. I am watching an angry, shifting river—angry over what the king is about to do.

The crowds flow toward the temple in an ever-condensing mass. I find myself moving with them, becoming a tributary to an expanding stream.

Having moved as close to the temple court as possible, I can see the platform on which King Hezekiah will sit to speak. It is impressively furnished with assorted priests, dignitaries, guards, and trumpeters. Unless I am mistaken, I see Isaiah, the city-bred prophet, and Micah, the farmer prophet, standing to the side. Both of them are uncompromising servants of Yahweh.

We wait.

At a given signal from the high priest, the trumpeters pierce the air with a call to attention. The king is about to appear.

Silence seizes the crowd.

THE JUDGMENT

In regal splendor, Hezekiah comes forward to be seated on his throne. Posted beside him is a priest who holds the bronze serpent and staff.

Hezekiah begins to speak. First he lifts his eyes heavenward and quotes part of the song Moses sang after God delivered his people from Pharaoh's grasp. "O Lord, there is no one like you among the gods. They can't match your glorious holiness. Your splendor overwhelms us. Your deeds are truly astonishing." Next, he faces us, and speaks in somber tones. "The Lord is ready to defend himself. He is going to judge the people. His judgment will especially target the elders and princes."

In a commanding voice, Hezekiah begins to recall Judah's history—going all the way back to the Exodus. He reminds us that our ancestors were slaves in Egypt and that God set them free. Hezekiah reviews the record of God's faithfulness during Israel's journey from Egypt to Sinai and from Sinai to Canaan. He reminds us of our ancestors' sorry pattern of complaining. The king joyfully reminds us of how God carried his people as a father carries a child. He reviews the conditions of the covenant God made with our father Abraham, and the covenant made at Sinai.

The king draws our attention to the fact that God called us to be peculiar among the nations. We were meant to love and serve the Holy One who made the heavens and the earth. He cannot be reduced to or compared with anything he made. He is the free, living God. The "gods" are nothing—just the products of sin and ignorance. The craftsmen who make the idols and all who trust in them will finally become like the lifeless things they worship.

Finally, Hezekiah stares at the bronze serpent and then at us. We are frozen under his gaze. Then his shocking judgment tumbles down: we are guilty of a sin even more hideous and deceptive than worshipping Baal. The bronze serpent is at the center of our transgression.

Hold on! I silently protest. I can accept God's judgment against Baal worship. But why should a sacred symbol we use for worshipping Yahweh—one created at his command—now be associated with sin? If the bronze serpent was one of God's gifts in the past, why should we fail to treat it that way now? Surely the king's careless words are good reason to suspect that his religious zeal has drifted into insanity.

Hezekiah continues by retelling the situation in the wilderness that brought the bronze serpent into existence. The serpent was an instrument of God's mercy. It was a symbol of his longsuffering willingness to forgive and heal. The repentant people were supposed to look beyond the physical object and place their trust in the Lord alone. The bronze serpent had no importance or healing power of its own. The only reason for keeping it was to constantly remind God's people of his unfailing guidance and grace. It should have helped renew their trust and worship of him.

But, Hezekiah instructs us, over time a lamentable and deceptive thing happened. Rather than worshipping the living God to whom the bronze serpent pointed, our ancestors began to worship the serpent itself. The physical object took God's place. That's idolatry. Hezekiah accuses us of zealously following in the steps of our ancestors. We have been duplicating their idolatry year after year. We pin God to a stick. To prove his charge, the king reminds us that we devotedly burn incense to the serpent.

Hezekiah cries out, "You and your ancestors have fallen prey to a most subtle sin. You abandoned your trust in Yahweh and placed it in one of his gifts." What was supposed to be a transparent sign became a concrete idol.

The king continues. The serpent-turned-idol must be destroyed. Only then can pure worship of the living God be restored.

With his gaze fixed on us, and with our attention riveted on our sin, Hezekiah asks, "What shall we do with the bronze serpent, you children of the covenant?"

Paralyzed silence follows.

Then from somewhere in the crowd a loud, anguished answer erupts: "Destroy the serpent! Destroy the idol! The Holy One of Israel, he alone is the living God!"

As chills ripple through my body, I recognize the voice as my own.

Getting Ready to Hear
(Chapter 5)

The ministry of the prophet Jeremiah lasted from 627 BC to sometime after 580 BC. He was witness to a defining era in Judah's history. His ministry began during the great revival led by King Josiah. He ministered during Judah's religious and political decline. He was present when Jerusalem and the temple were destroyed in 587-586. Against Jeremiah's will, survivors took him and Baruch, Jeremiah's secretary, to Egypt where Jeremiah died.

Jeremiah addressed many abuses of the covenant that God made with his people. One of them was the insidious belief that God had unconditionally promised David and Solomon that a descendent of David would always sit upon Judah's throne. Many people took this to mean that no matter how they lived, God was bound by oath to protect Jerusalem and the temple. Another abuse was that God's well-being depended upon the temple's existence. The people treated God like some pagan deity whose existence relied upon his temple's safety. Yahweh, the people had been taught, could not permit destruction of his temple without jeopardizing himself. He didn't transcend his temple. He was trapped. Old Testament theologian Dennis Bratcher says that one of the dangers associated with building the temple in the first place was that Israel's dynamic relationship with the living God might be reduced to a physical place—to a predictable status quo.[4]

Unlike the gods of the ancient Canaanite population who were bound to sacred places, the God of the patriarchs is not bound to a particular place. He is a journeying God, a shepherd who leads his people into new paths. To serve and live with this God requires becoming a pilgrim people. There is a big difference between a sedentary faith and a nomadic faith.

The Baal of the trapped God incarnates itself repeatedly. The notion that God is locked into promises that release us from responsibility or that his own well-being somehow hinges on the existence of a place, nation, or institution is a Baal that never retires.

In this chapter Hananiah's voice carries the narrative. He figures in the Book of Jeremiah (28:1-16) as an opponent of the prophet. Uriel, Menahem, and Ze'ev are fictional.

The pertinent scriptures are 2 Kings 22—25; 2 Chron. 34—36; Isa. 66:1-2; the Book of Jeremiah. See also the stark allegory of the destruction of Jerusalem in Ezek. 24:1-14.

5

THE GOD WHO CAN'T BE TRAPPED

Night had shrouded the besieged city. But it could not cover the sounds of fear and suffering—the screams of mothers unable to feed their starving children; the whimpers of ragged beggars creeping from shadow to shadow; and the shuffling feet of demoralized soldiers plodding by. The chill of impending disaster hung in the air.

But for me there was reason to celebrate. King Zedekiah had permitted the princes to put my hated enemy to death. Mud in the bottom of a cistern was now sucking away his life. His hated prophecies, his claim to speak for Yahweh, and all his accusations against me were dying with him. So we rejoiced. My fellow prophets and I sipped our hoarded wine; the Babylonians seemed far away.

My name is Hananiah. Perhaps you have heard of me. I was a leader among the professional prophets connected to the king's court. My assignment was to give the king a fresh word from the Lord. But I knew in my heart that I had no such word. Even if I had, I would not have had the courage to deliver it. Court prophets habitually assured the king and the populace that Yahweh was bound by oath to protect Jerusalem and the temple—no matter what. We were willing to say anything to make people believe peace and safety were on the horizon. Even after the Babylonians crossed into Judah, we confidently assured the harried people that God would restore the good old days of national glory.

The *Traitor* had long been my enemy. He was always contradicting my optimistic prophecies. He charged that my credentials were bogus. The "visions" of the court prophets, he insisted, were nothing but damning lies. Truthfully, I knew his accusations were accurate. But the king and populace were on our side.

Some of us had suffered the *Traitor's* rebukes for over thirty years. We hoped that before the evening's end, word of his death would reach us. Gleeful anticipation mingled with the warmth of the wine and shielded us against the cold.

THE TRAITOR AND KING JOSIAH

Conversation that evening naturally focused on the *Traitor.* Uriel, one of the older prophets, recalled that the *Traitor* first appeared during the thirteenth year of King Josiah's reign. A young man at the time, the *Traitor* came from a priestly family in the village of Anathoth.

In between sips of wine, Uriel reminded us of Josiah's efforts to rid Judah of pagan influences and restore the worship of Yahweh. He had his work cut out for him. Manasseh, Josiah's grandfather, spent most of his thirty-five-year reign reinstating the pagan abominations his father, Hezekiah, had struggled to eliminate.

Amon, Josiah's father, zealously continued Manasseh's pagan program. After reigning for only two years, he was assassinated.

That was what Josiah inherited. He was eight years old when he began to reign, and reigned for thirty-one years. Early, Josiah began to seek the God of David. In the twelfth year he began the long and difficult process of purging Judah and Jerusalem of deeply embedded paganism. He began by getting rid of all signs of Assyrian control. Josiah was encouraged by Babylonia's successful rebellion against Assyria.

Uriel shielded himself against the chill, took more wine, and remarked that the older ones among us would never forget the discovery of the Book of the Law in the temple. During the eighteenth year of Josiah's reign, workers who were repairing the temple accidentally stumbled upon it. Josiah's secretary sent the scroll to the king, who requested that it be read. As Josiah listened, he was so overwhelmed he tore his garments. He was horrified by the contrast between God's will as revealed in the Book of the Law and the way his people were living.

Josiah urgently summoned the people to the temple for a great covenant renewal service. Like the king, the people were overwhelmed when the scroll was read. They immediately reaffirmed their covenant with Yahweh.

THE GREAT REVIVAL

Uriel distinctly recalled seeing the *Traitor* out in the streets, urging support for the revival. He had preached that the Mosaic Covenant should be the standard for Judah's piety.

The Book of the Law became a blueprint for the reforms that followed. The vitality of Judah's covenant with Yahweh had to be renewed almost from the foundation up. Josiah abolished Canaanite Baal worship, worship of Ishtar (the Assyrian Queen of Heaven), and worship of other deities such as Molech (an Ammonite deity to whom children are sacrificed). All pagan objects found in the temple were removed and burned. Child sacrifice, sacred prostitution associated with fertility cults, and consultation with mediums and wizards were outlawed.

Of special importance, Uriel recalled, was that Josiah tried to purify Judah's faith by concentrating all worship in the Jerusalem temple. This would eliminate the pagan practices that had crept into the outlying shrines devoted to worshipping Yahweh.

Along with the great religious reforms came a rising tide of national self-confidence. It seemed that Judah was about to enter a golden age similar to the glorious days of King David.

THE GREAT COLLAPSE

Ze'ev, a young understudy just beginning to learn the ways of court prophets, broke in, "So what became of the great revival?"

Uriel paused and calmly answered, "It collapsed—collapsed like a cake carelessly removed from the oven."

"Why?" Ze'ev asked—half in disbelief.

"Listen carefully," Uriel urged. "The answer might leave you puzzled. The immediate cause for the collapse made no sense at all."

Josiah's political and military successes were made possible by Assyria's weakness. Babylon, one of the countries Assyria had bullied, fought for and gained independence. It was gaining power. Egypt was also rising from the ashes.

In a shocking twist, Egypt decided to assist Assyria. It figured that Babylon would become the new military threat. So Pharaoh Necho decided to restrain Babylon and prop up Assyria. Josiah, on the other hand, decided to support Babylon. He planned to win Babylon's favor by trapping Necho at the Megiddo Pass on his way to aid Assyria.

With the revival in full swing, and nationalism running high, Josiah engaged Necho. Chaos. The battle quickly turned against Judah. Josiah was wounded and hustled back to Jerusalem where he died. Great national mourning followed.

Not yet forty years old, the energizing center of the revival was dead. Judah became Egypt's vassal, as Necho marched on to fight Babylonia at Carchemish.

Josiah's death shook Judah's morale like a reed shaken by the winter wind. Disillusionment was overwhelming. How could God have encouraged the revival and then permitted Josiah's death? Were not wealth and security supposed to follow as benefits of Judah's return to righteousness? What good is a God who can't protect his own people? Most of the populace decided they had erred grievously by deserting their pagan gods. "Maybe it is not too late to recover their favor."

I interjected that the *Traitor* deserted the revival also, but not because of Josiah's death. He said the peoples' return to the Mosaic Covenant had been very shallow. They had not plowed the untilled ground of their hard hearts. The people, the *Traitor* charged, had treated Yahweh like a pagan deity; they had worshipped him only for the benefits they expected to receive. He preached that reciprocated love between God and his people—the real content of covenant—had escaped them completely.

Within twenty years from Josiah's death, all traces of revival had been scrubbed from Judah's public memory.

Menahem, a grizzled old prophet hardened by years of lies, had listened quietly. He could no longer restrain himself. He took over the telling. After Josiah's death, his son Jehoahaz reigned for three months. The Egyptians dumped him and placed Jehoiakim, another of Josiah's sons, on the throne. He ruled as Egypt's puppet for his first four years. Jehoiakim was cruel and selfish. To pay Egypt its tribute, he taxed the people heavily. To build his luxurious palaces, he subjected the people to forced labor.

Jehoiakim restored the paganism Josiah had tried to eliminate. The people didn't need much encouragement. Disillusioned over Josiah's death and God's "failure" to deliver prosperity and security, they enthusiastically picked up their former ways.

THE SERMON

As the pagan tide rose, Menahem continued, the *Traitor* could no longer contain his wrath. He had watched as people streamed into the temple to fulfill the formalities of worship. He accused them of using worship of Yahweh as a cover for their sins. Early in Jehoiakim's reign, the *Traitor* came to the temple and preached an inflammatory sermon.

He told the people that their religious leaders—including the court prophets—had sold them a damnable lie about the temple and its rituals. They were being told that God was actually located in the temple and that his being there guaranteed the temple's survival. The temple, in turn, would forever guarantee Judah's security—no matter how the people lived. God's own well-being depended on the temple's survival.

The *Traitor* charged that the people and their religious leaders were treating Yahweh as just another dependent pagan deity. They had reduced him to the dimensions of a building and its ritual.

Yahweh, the *Traitor* proclaimed, is not like the pagan gods. He is the free and living God who transcends his own temple. He would still be God even if the temple were to disappear. He can't be trapped in a building. Don't count on the temple as protection against the consequences of apostasy. The temple is no guarantee that God is with us and no refuge for hiding sin.

The *Traitor* preached that God's patience with Judah had run out. He was sick of seeing people chase after other gods and then come to the temple with the smell of Baal incense still clinging to their clothes. Unless the people were willing to obey the voice of the Lord, and walk in all his ways, the temple was meaningless.

He contradicted one of our treasured dogmas. We believed God had promised David and Solomon that He would forever maintain a descendent of David on the throne. We thought the oath guaranteed the existence of the temple and Jerusalem. The *Traitor* said we had turned the promise into a trap for God. We had ignored an essential condition of the promise: "*If* you will obey my voice and keep my covenant, *then* . . ."

As the *Traitor* was finishing his sermon, Menahem angrily recalled, he became more extreme. If the people refused to repent and walk according to all God's ways, then God would destroy the temple. He would also destroy Jerusalem and make it the object of ridicule among the nations. Judah would go into exile.

Treason! What other conclusion could one draw? "*Traitor*" should be the preacher's name.

Those who heard the sermon responded with shock and animosity. The *Traitor's* death was enthusiastically demanded. He would have been executed had not Ahikam—an influential prince—intervened. The *Traitor* went into hiding.

THE BABYLONIANS

As Menahem paused to stretch and drink more wine, Uriel—eyes now bleary—picked up the story. He recalled that during the fourth year of Jehoiakim's reign, the Babylonians defeated Pharaoh Necho at the Battle of Carchemish. Judah soon came under Babylonian domination.

That same year—about eight years before the Babylonians first invaded Judah—the *Traitor* recorded all his messages on a scroll. Baruch, the *Traitor's* secretary, read the scroll in the temple. It warned that Yahweh was going to pour out his wrath against Judah. The Babylonians—coming from the North—would be God's instrument of punishment. Upon hearing this, the people were horrified. The scroll so angered King Jehoiakim that the *Traitor* and his secretary fled into hiding.

About five years later, after the Babylonians and Egyptians had bloodied each other in battle, Jehoiakim refused to pay tribute to Babylon. Infuriated, the Babylonians prepared to invade and punish Judah. But before they arrived, Jehoiakim died and left his eighteen-year-old son, Jehoiachin, to absorb the Babylonian invasion. As part of their punishment, the Babylonians stripped the temple of its royal treasures. The king, his queen mother, and the leading citizens—the nobility, artisans, and high military officers—were taken to Babylon as exiles.

As disastrous as the invasion was, we the court prophets were quick to point out that the temple and Jerusalem were still standing. Part of the *Traitor's* prophecy had come true. But the most important parts—destruction of the temple and the ruin of Jerusalem—had not. The *Traitor* had been wrong.

Before leaving Judah, the Babylonians placed Josiah's twenty-one-year-old son, Mattaniah, on the throne and changed his name to Zedekiah. He reigned for eleven years. The young princes wanted to join Egypt in a rebellion against Babylon. But Zedekiah resisted. The court prophets supported the princes. Uriel recalled how we beat the drums of nationalism and preached our old sermons about God's guarantee of protection.

The wine was beginning to slur Uriel's speech and cloud his mind. Menahem was fighting sleep. So I took over. The rest of the story had particular significance for me anyway.

During those years, the *Traitor* came out of hiding and resumed his preaching—always said he didn't even want to be a preacher. In Zedekiah's fourth year, Egypt sent envoys to seek Judah's aid in rebelling against Babylon. The *Traitor* opposed it.

One day, while the Egyptian envoys were still in town, the *Traitor* showed up in the streets wearing a yoke around his neck—said God told him to do it. He preached that it was God's will for Judah and the nations to submit to Babylon. Better to submit to Babylon's yoke than for Jerusalem to be destroyed. "If you serve the king of Babylon, you will live and not die," he shouted. His "yoke" and preaching were clearly treasonous. He even wore his "Babylonian yoke" into the temple—the very house of the Lord, his guarantee of our security.

I confronted the *Traitor* in the temple, silenced him, and calmed the people. I assured them the temple would keep them safe. God would never permit its destruction. I told them that within two years, God would completely restore everything the Babylonians had stolen. Then I stripped the yoke from the *Traitor*'s neck and broke it. Yahweh, I proclaimed, would strip the yoke of Babylon from the necks of all the nations.

THE CATASTROPHE

I was wrong.

A little more than two years ago, King Zedekiah rejected the *Traitor*'s counsel and signed on with the Egyptians in a second round of rebellion.

The decision was a catastrophic blunder. The Egyptians retreated and left us exposed. The Babylonians struck unmercifully. They captured our fortified cities and then laid siege to Jerusalem.

During the siege, the *Traitor* declared that anyone who remained in the city would die by sword, famine, or disease. "Flee, and surrender to the Babylonians."

That was the final straw. The *Traitor* was destroying the morale of the people and the army. *He had to die.* One week ago, the princes and some soldiers seized him. They placed ropes under his arms and lowered him into a cistern. As soon as the ropes were removed, the *Traitor* began to sink into the muck.

That was the "good news" that launched our gleeful celebration.

Now, a bitter sickness of soul haunts me as the story ends. Unspeakable suffering plagued the city as the siege wore on. Starvation stalked the streets. With the city's food, water, and defenses depleted, resistance collapsed.

Four days ago the Babylonians breached Jerusalem's walls. For two years, their desire for vengeance had festered. Now it burst like a ripened boil. The Babylonians stripped the temple of its remaining gold, silver, and bronze. Young men who had fled there for safety were killed. Royal officials paid for their rebellion in the coinage of execution. Then the temple was *burned* as a sacrifice to Babylonian vengeance. The city—including its grand houses—suffered the same fate. Hungry fires have raged for three days. The bodies of soldiers and citizens now litter the streets. The smell of death is in the air. Bursts of wailing punctuate the chaos. The city's once-proud walls are being demolished. Looting now complete, nothing of value remains. The Davidic lineage is finished.

THE HOPE?

I stand outside the city—clothed in numbing, inexpressible grief. My once haughty spirit has been crushed. My superficial religion has been discredited. Plagued by my pointless life, I wander aimlessly among the shattered survivors. One moment I glance back at the burning city. The next moment I gaze eastward toward Babylon, for I am going into exile. Only the poorest of the land and some local leaders—such as Gedaliah—will remain.

On the night before the Babylonians breached the walls, I received astonishing news. The *Traitor* had not died! Zedekiah had sent Ebed-melech—one of his servants—to rescue him.

Jeremiah yet lives!

As I begin my journey into exile, I am haunted by a disturbing—but hopeful—question: "Does Yahweh still live?"

Getting Ready to Hear
(Chapter 6)

Cyrus the Great, king of Persia, sealed the fate of the Babylonian Empire in 539 BC. As head of the new world power, he initiated a policy (538 BC) that permitted captives to return to their homelands and rebuild their temples. His policy directly affected the Jews—exiles for 59 years. The first deportation to Babylon had occurred in 597 BC, the second in 587 BC. In years to come, an undetermined number returned to Jerusalem in four stages. The return marked the beginning of postexilic Judaism. Those who returned eventually rebuilt the temple and city walls. Work on the temple began in 521 BC and was completed in 516 BC. The city walls were restored in 443 BC under Nehemiah's leadership. The rebuilt temple marked the beginning of second temple Judaism.

Those monumental events and the restoration of Jerusalem's religious institutions changed Judaism in important ways and prepared it for subsequent challenges—from the Greeks and the Romans. Postexilic Judaism expressed itself in diverse forms, all of which revolved around careful obedience to God's will expressed in Torah (Law). Everyone agreed the Law was given to Israel because God had chosen and entered into covenant with it. The Jews worshipped one God and carefully guarded against idolatry. Certain dietary regulations, such as not eating pork, were observed. Males were circumcised as a clear demarcation between Jews and outsiders. The Sabbath was scrupulously observed.

The differences in postexilic Judaism revolved around how best to obey the Torah's regulations. Some adopted a measure of accommodation to the surrounding culture. Others, in the interest of purity, turned inward and built a protective "hedge around the Torah" (Mishnah, Aboth 1:1)—eventually composed of 613 commandments (*mitzvot*). They embraced a strictly separatist posture. Eventually the Pharisees would emerge and be numbered here.

The reforms of Ezra and Nehemiah expressed the conviction that God had chosen Israel for a special relationship requiring strict Torah observance. Israel was to be a holy people, fit to live in a holy city. Most broadly, Torah meant living in obedient response to the voice of the Lord and walking in his path as had been made clear in his deeds and words. Torah had always included specific guidance for obeying the covenant. But after the Exile, Torah acquired a new rigidity of ethical and religious boundaries, which distanced the Jews from their neighbors. Determination to be holy and not repeat Israel's descent into idolatry and apostasy motivated this form of Judaism.

One threat to the restoration of worship and Torah observance came from ideas picked up in Babylon that were foreign to the Mosaic faith. Another threat was that many exiles had married non-Israelites who worshipped Mesopotamian and Canaanite gods. The danger associated with the vigorous effort to cleanse the covenant people from all foreign pollutions was that Judaism would adopt a narrow and exclusive, defensive and rigid—even condescending—attitude toward persons outside the purity boundaries. Men, not God, might come to decide with whom God should associate and who should receive his mercy—"God under wraps." This chapter uses the experiences of a fictional pious Jew—Shaphan (a family name in the Book of Jeremiah)—to examine the contours of the Baal we shall call "God under wraps."

As the story unfolds, keep in mind that the Book of the Law of Moses referred to in association with Ezra is the Book of Deuteronomy.

The pertinent scriptures are the Books of Ezra, Nehemiah, 2 Chronicles (chap. 36), Jonah, and Zechariah (chaps. 1—8). After reading the chapter, read Isa. 55; 56:1-8.

— 6 —

GOD UNDER WRAPS?

The *vision* has left me startled and perplexed. I'll tell the story to you.

Three days ago I was engaged in the evening service (*'Arvit*) of daily prayers. I had solemnly joined in praying the opening blessing—the Shema: "Hear, Israel, the Lord is our God, the Lord is One." Suddenly, an angel appeared to me in a *vision*. He called me by name and summoned me to hear the story of a strange prophet.

I am Shaphan—a Jew. I was once a successful merchant in Nippur, a Babylonian city. That was my livelihood. Preserving the purity of the Mosaic faith is my passion.

I'll share some events that led up to the *vision*. That will help you understand my puzzlement.

My wife and I were among the exiles who returned to Jerusalem under the leadership of Nehemiah—cupbearer to the Persian king Artaxerxes I. Nehemiah had received news of the hard times residents of Jerusalem were enduring. He was moved to tears and mourning. Nehemiah received permission from the king to go to Jerusalem to provide assistance. I happily transferred my business to my sons and prepared to accompany him.

One cause for distress in Jerusalem was that its walls, towers, and gates still lay in ruins. Weeds grew between the once-proud stones. Jackals and rodents ran over them, punctuating the tragedy. The tumbled walls made the residents vulnerable. Nehemiah wanted to rebuild the walls and construct new gates. Not only did the king grant permission but he also provided letters of royal authorization that could be presented to neighboring governors who might challenge Nehemiah's mission.

Our arrival in Jerusalem was 120 years after the destruction of the first temple and approximately 70 years after construction and dedication of a second temple. The prophet Haggai had encouraged the people in the rebuilding. Unlike the Babylonians, the Persians encouraged exiles to return home and rebuild their centers of worship. They provided monetary support for reconstruction. We Jews knew that Cyrus, the first Persian king, had even returned sacred vessels the Babylonians had taken from the Jerusalem temple.

A NEED FOR REVIVAL

I have been told that great rejoicing surrounded the second temple's dedication. A memorable Passover and Feast of Unleavened Bread followed. But in time, zeal that characterized those events declined. Eventually the hearts of the people were no longer in their worship. They were just going through the motions.

Then God sent a prophet named Malachi. He urged the people to return to sincere worship. He accused them of dishonoring Yahweh in their temple offerings and sacrifices. They were placing polluted foods on the altar and sacrificing their blind, lame, and sickly animals. Malachi said the priests had failed to safeguard the Law.

People complained that serving God didn't bring any noticeable material benefits. But they thought evildoers were succeeding quite well.

Malachi heard it all and told the people it would be better to close the temple than to turn worship into a charade. Yahweh, he said, deserves the best. He shocked the people by saying that many Gentiles showed God more honor than they were demonstrating.

REBUILDING THE WALLS

Later, when Nehemiah and those of us who came with him arrived, renewal was sorely needed. Community, founded upon a love for God and neighbor, had to be restored. Given the people's downcast spirit, and their limited resources, rebuilding the walls posed a major challenge.

Nehemiah carefully assessed the needs and rallied the people. He grouped priests, nobles, officials, and families into teams. He assigned sections of the wall, the towers, and the gates to various teams. His rallying theme was: "Let's all work together and rebuild these walls." A militia was organized to protect the workers.

Soon, Nehemiah's leadership skills were put to the test. Sanballat—governor of Samaria—and his allies hurled derision and accusations at the people. They laughed and called us puny Jews. They accused us of plotting against the king of Persia.

Some of the better-off Jews exploited some of the people by charging them crippling interest rates for loans. Some Jews mingled with the opponents—even to the extent of marriage.

Nehemiah responded by enforcing a strict policy of exclusion. He sternly enforced the prohibition against intermarriage. Only those who were of pure Jewish ancestry could be recognized as authentic Jews. To be included in the community, they must be faithful to the Torah and the temple, and they must strictly observe the Sabbath. Nehemiah was keenly aware of the threat of syncretism—mixing religions. He even banished a priest for marrying a daughter of Sanballat.

I applauded Nehemiah's actions. Israel must be a "peculiar people," not polluted by the nations. We must build a fence around the Torah.

We were all amazed that rebuilding the walls and towers, and constructing and mounting the new gates, took only fifty-two days.

THE ARRIVAL OF EZRA

About twenty years after our arrival, an event occurred that was to have a profound impact upon the Jews in Palestine. Ezra, a priest and scribe skilled in the Law of God, arrived from Babylonia. A caravan of exiles came along with him. Artaxerxes II had commissioned Ezra to provide religious instruction for the people. He directed Ezra to build upon Nehemiah's reforms. The king even provided financial support for Ezra's mission.

A GREAT COVENANT RENEWAL

Ezra brought with him the Book of the Law of Moses. When the time for the Feast of Tabernacles arrived, the people assembled as one person and asked Ezra to bring the book so that he could reveal its message to them. We planned to congregate before sunrise in the square before the Jerusalem Water Gate.

When the time arrived, anticipation was great. My wife and I arrived early. We claimed a space near the platform where Ezra would stand. As he mounted the platform, the people stood at fixed attention. He opened the book and blessed the Lord. Then, as one person, we answered, "Amen, Amen." We lifted our hands, bowed our heads, and worshipped God.

Ezra began to read. He read from early morning till noon. He read in Hebrew—a language we former exiles no longer understood. While we were in Babylonia, we began to speak Aramaic—the language of administration and communication for the Assyrians, Babylonians, and Persians. The Levites, who understood Hebrew and Aramaic and who were responsible for explaining Israel's faith, stood at Ezra's side. They translated the Hebrew into Aramaic.

Overwhelmed, the people wept in sorrow as Ezra concluded. He told us not to weep. It was a day holy to the Lord. "Celebrate; don't grieve," he said. "Rejoicing in the Lord will be your strength."

On the following day, we began to celebrate the Feast of Tabernacles as the Law directed. We cut branches and built booths in which to live during the seven-day festival. The feast reached an astonishing climax when Ezra led the people in a solemn act of covenant renewal.

In preparation for the renewal, we separated ourselves from all foreigners. As a sign of repentance, we dressed in sackcloth. With Ezra acting as our covenant mediator, we confessed our sins and the sins of our fathers. The Book of the Law of Moses was read, and all of us worshipped the Lord. In a lengthy prayer, Ezra confessed Israel's faith. He addressed his prayer to the gracious God who keeps covenant and practices steadfast love.

Next, all the people solemnly promised that we would carefully observe the Lord's ordinances and statutes. We said: "We are placing this covenant in writing. To eliminate any question, our princes, Levites, and priests will put their seal on it."

One thing all of us promised was that we would never invite apostasy by giving our daughters in marriage to non-Jews. We would never receive the daughters of Gentiles for our sons. Ezra even demanded that those of us who had married non-Israelite wives divorce them.

From now on, strict conformity to the Law—obligations about worship and social relations within the covenant community—would become the basis for God's holy people. Our obedience was to follow as joyous response to our gracious God.

NEVER AGAIN

In the following weeks, the grand covenant renewal prompted me to reflect on the history of our people—especially why catastrophe had descended. I recalled that even as exile was beginning, the prophet Ezekiel told the Jews in Babylon that their sorrow was the bitter harvest of persistent faithlessness. Israel and Judah had acted like twin harlots. They squandered God's selection of them as his people. They forgot that God meant for them to be a peculiar people—separated to the Lord. They mingled with and adopted the ways of polluted nations.

I am sure you can understand. That must never happen again! The descent into harlotry must not be repeated. The holiness of Yahweh must be reflected in what we wear, where we live, what and with whom we eat, and with whom we fellowship. The boundaries that mark God's elect and holy community must be impenetrable. Those on the outside and those on the inside must be carefully distinguished. All unclean elements must be rooted out.

Genealogy, circumcision, strict observance of the Sabbath, and minute observance of the Law of God will distinguish between the pure and the impure.

Saying that foreigners who do not love and observe the Law are a "lesser breed" is not saying too much. Their wickedness makes them fit targets for disdain and exclusion.

Even within Israel diverse levels of purity must be maintained. Levites, for example, should not marry proselytes—

Gentile converts to Judaism—lest they decrease their degree of purity or holiness.

We must remember that all God's designs focus on preserving the elect community. Yes, with election comes responsibility, but also privilege. Clearly identifying Israel's enemies will be another way for us to distinguish between sinners and the righteous. Enemies of Israel are enemies of righteousness. God will punish them in due course.

THE VISION

With others, I had just begun evening prayers by quoting the Shema blessing—Israel's central affirmation. The final words would have been: "I am the Lord, your God. I am the One who delivered you from Egyptian bondage. You have no other God."

At that point, I heard my name being called, called in a voice like none I had ever heard. Trembling, I looked in the voice's direction. There stood an angel of the Lord—bathed in the glory of the heavenly realm. Overwhelmed, I fell on my face as though dead. The hand of the Lord had come upon me.

The angel commanded: "Give ear, Shaphan. The Lord has sent me to show you a vision and explain to you the story of a prophet named Jonah. Make ready to receive the word of the Lord."

Feebly, I responded: "Blessed are you, Eternal One, our God, Sovereign of the universe. Make known your holy name in the midst of your people."

Immediately, the angel transported me to the scene of a raging sea. I saw in the midst of the sea a small ship—tossing and threatening to break up. On its deck the terrified mariners were huddled. Through the storm, I could hear them crying to their gods for mercy. Then, I watched as they threw the ship's cargo into the churning waters, trying to lighten and thus save the ship.

Upon hearing the mariners, I was repulsed by their pagan prayers.

"Shaphan," the angel commanded, "look down into the hold of the ship. What do you see?"

I looked. And behold, a man was lying there, fast asleep like a lamb in a shepherd's arms.

Astonished by the sharp contrast between the raging sea and the sleeping man, I asked, "Who is this man?"

"He is a prophet of the Lord. His name is Jonah."

"Why is he here in the midst of this storm?"

"He is running away from the Lord."

"But that makes no sense," I protested. "Why would the Lord's prophet run away?"

"Because he fiercely opposes bearing the message God gave him to proclaim."

Half in disbelief, I queried, "And what is that message?"

"Give heed, Shaphan. The Lord came to Jonah, saying, 'Arise. Go to the great and famous city of Nineveh. Preach as a prophet against the city and its people. Their unsurpassed wickedness demands my attention and action.'"

At the mention of Nineveh, my anger raced. That great city had been the capital of the Assyrians. They were the wicked and ruthless people who destroyed the Northern Kingdom and threatened to destroy Judah. My hatred for them knew no bounds. "Let God's wrath fall upon them. Amen!"

I was greatly puzzled. Any prophet of the Lord would delight to announce God's judgment upon the Ninevites. But Nineveh lay in the East; Jonah was proceeding west.

"Why?" I asked.

"Because Jonah refused to deliver the word of the Lord. He went down to Joppa, paid the fare, and sailed for Tarshish. He tried to run away from God. The voyage had barely begun when God hurled this great wind upon the sea."

I watched as the ship's captain accosted Jonah for sleeping. "Get up," I heard him say. "Plead with your God. Maybe he is the only one powerful enough to calm this raging sea."

The mariners knew that a god had sent the storm to punish some terrible offense. As the ship tossed, they cast lots to learn on whose account the terrible evil had descended. The lot fell upon Jonah.

I strained to hear as the mariners plied Jonah with questions. "Who are you? What evil did you commit to endanger our lives? Who are your people?"

Jonah responded that he was a Hebrew and that he feared the God of Heaven who created the ocean and the dry land. He told them that he had disobeyed the Lord and was fleeing his presence.

I wondered, "How could anyone—especially a prophet—hope to flee God's presence?" Then I heard Jonah tell the mariners to toss him overboard. "Only then," he said, "will the storm cease."

At first, the mariners refused. Out of compassion for Jonah, they struggled to bring the ship back to port. Their efforts were for naught; the sea grew worse. I listened as the mariners prayed to Jonah's God, asking him to spare their lives. "O Lord, you have done what you wanted to do, and no one could resist you."

Then they pitched Jonah overboard. As soon as his feet touched the water, the storm ceased. I saw the fear of the Lord grip the mariners. Then they did something that caught me completely off guard. They offered a sacrifice to the Lord and made vows to him.

The angel saw my surprise and asked, "Shaphan, why have the sacrifice and vow surprised you? Is it because these pagans are among those you say are excluded from God's mercy? Have they not shown more honor to God than did Jonah? Did they not extend more mercy to Jonah than Jonah extended to them?"

While I was unsuccessfully fumbling for answers, the angel commanded, "Behold, Shaphan, what do you see?"

I strained to answer, but could not. "You know, sir," I mumbled.

"Jonah has been swallowed by a great fish. Instead of permitting him to drown, God has shown mercy. He has provided aquatic quarters."

Never had I witnessed a dwelling like that.

For three days, the great fish hosted the truant prophet. I listened to the sounds of the sea and the sounds of the great fish. At first, Jonah said nothing. Then, suddenly he prayed a psalm of thanksgiving: "In desperation I cried out to the Lord. He answered me. From the region of darkness and the threat of death I cried to the Lord. The gracious Lord heard my prayer."

While I was rejoicing over Jonah's psalm, the angel asked, "Shaphan, son of man, does it not bother you that the prophet rejoices in God's undeserved mercy but will not extend mercy to others unless he thinks they deserve it?"

I wanted to explain to the angel that only by avoiding wicked people can Israel hope to remain pure. I wanted to tell him that election requires rigid separation. But before I could instruct the angel, the great fish vomited Jonah upon the shore.

I wondered, "What will the prophet do now?" An answer came quickly. Jonah began an express trip east to Nineveh, where he would proclaim the word of the Lord.

Then, the angel transported me to Nineveh. Renewed resentment against the city raced through my mind as its massive walls and gates came into view.

I watched warily as Jonah began to inventory the city's wickedness. His righteous rage now sufficiently stoked, Jonah began to preach: "In forty days I will destroy Nineveh." I heard and blessed the Lord: "The people whom God loves will benefit greatly; they will inherit the earth. But the evil people God curses won't stand a chance. God will eliminate them."

I was unprepared for the shocking turn the story took next. It has destabilized my understanding of God's ways. I am puzzled about how to pray, how to live, what it means to be God's people—in short, how to proceed from here.

The cause of my shock? The people of Nineveh—that most wicked of cities—obeyed the word of the Lord. I watched as the king himself led the people in repentance. He arose from his throne, removed his robe, and covered himself with sackcloth. As the ultimate expression of repentance, he sat in ashes. The angel asked, "Shaphan, have you ever done that?"

I listened as the king's heralds proclaimed in the city, "No one is going eat or drink water. This includes people and beasts of burden, cattle and sheep. They must not so much as taste food or drink water. Men and beasts must be covered with sackcloth. Let everyone cry out to God in repentance. Let them stop doing evil things such as using their hands for violence. Who knows, maybe God will hear our prayers and turn away his anger. Maybe we will not perish."

The king's petition sounded like one the prophet Ezekiel might have instructed the exiles in Babylon to pray.

Here, the *vision* took a very dark turn. When God heard the Ninevites repenting and saw them turning from their wicked ways, he withdrew his sentence of destruction.

Jonah exploded in anger. God had betrayed him. What Jonah feared most had happened. By contrast, the angel's face glowed with delight. Did he somehow think God had acted in character?

Seated outside the city, Jonah asked the Lord to let him die. He would rather die than see God behave as he had. Ah! How I empathized with Jonah.

As he waited for death, and watched to see what would happen to the city, Jonah built a booth for protection against the sun. I thought it strange; why protect yourself if you want to die?

The angel directed my gaze to the ground. There, shooting up, was a castor-oil plant. It grew rapidly until it was large enough to give shade to the prophet. Jonah, who had moments ago wanted to die, rejoiced over his "new companion."

But when the sun rose the next day, Jonah was alarmed to discover that a worm had destroyed the plant. Its death sent him into deep mourning. The loss was so distressing that Jonah again asked the Lord to let him die. Even I thought his response too extreme.

QUESTIONS

All of a sudden I heard a new voice. Its questions to Jonah let me know it was the voice of the Lord. He asked, "Is it good for you to be angry over the untimely death of a plant?"

"Of course," Jonah replied. "I am angry enough to die."

At this point, my puzzlement about the *vision* compounded. But the angel's face revealed understanding and approval.

God spoke again: "How foolish! Here you are, grieving over dead vegetation. You didn't plant it, and you certainly didn't make it grow. It sprouted one night and died the next. So what's wrong with me accepting the Ninevites' repentance? There are over a hundred and twenty thousand persons in Nineveh. Why shouldn't I be willing to forgive them?"

I anxiously awaited Jonah's response. I needed his answer as instruction, for Jonah's problem was mine also.

The *vision* ended.

Anxiously, I turned to the angel—his inquisitive gaze now fixed upon me—and I asked, "How did Jonah respond to God?"

Before the angel could answer, I muttered to myself, "A free, unbounded God? That could be very dangerous."

The angel smiled and asked, "Shaphan, what had Jonah forgotten?"

I searched for an answer, came up blank, and asked, "Sir, you know?"

"Jonah forgot that if God had applied the rule of strict punishment to the wayward prophet as he expected God to apply it to the Ninevites, he would still be in the fish's belly. He also had forgotten that if God were not merciful to those who don't deserve mercy, the Jews would still be in Egypt's belly."

The angel said, "And you, Shaphan, seem to have forgotten that if God had applied 'Jonah's rule' to the Jews in exile, as you are in danger of applying to 'outsiders,' they would still be in Babylon's belly."

While I was struggling to appear coherent, the angel continued: "Shaphan, child of the covenant, go and learn. Learn from the prophet Isaiah what it means for Israel to be a 'missionary people'—'a light to the nations.'"

With that, he was gone.

Getting Ready to Hear
(Chapter 7)

The notion of a suffering (crucified) Messiah was foreign to what Jews expected of the anticipated Messiah. As early as 200 BC (the date is uncertain) the Aramaic paraphrase (the Targum Jonathan*) of Isa. 52:13—53:12 removed suffering from the role of the Servant described there, but said, "my servant the Messiah" will be exalted (52:13). Before Paul's conversion he opposed the young Church for preaching that the crucified Jesus was the Messiah. Later when he tried to preach Christ to the Jews, most of them rejected the message of a crucified and risen Messiah (Greek, *Christos*). They said the claim was scandalous (1 Cor. 1:22-25). "Messiah" and "suffering" were believed to be mutually exclusive terms.

Were the Jews the last to refuse to associate suffering with the Redeemer? Absolutely not! Through the centuries many Christians have crafted for themselves a Christ and a form of discipleship packed with happy benefits but void of suffering. Unlike many Christians in some parts of the world, where being Christian invites persecution and even martyrdom, many of us in the West are tempted by a form of discipleship described as "entitlement Christianity."

---

*After the return from Babylonian Exile the Aramaic language became the vernacular among the Jews of Palestine. It was the medium in which Jesus communicated. The Targums (from *targem*, to interpret) were Aramaic paraphrases of the Hebrew Scriptures. The eventual written versions arose from the custom of orally repeating and explaining the Hebrew sacred text in the synagogue in Aramaic. Targum Jonathan, which had its origin in Israel, is the official eastern (Babylonian) Targum to the prophets.

"Entitlement Christianity" scrubs "the way of the cross" from Christian discipleship. It makes of Christ a nanny protector who must rid life of danger, disappointment, and aggravation. To gain our allegiance Christ must shower us with the pleasant and pleasing. The mantra is, "It is my 'right' to be happy, and Christ must make it so." *Happiness* is tethered to shifting circumstances; *joy* is anchored in the peace of Christ and Christian hope.

We call this popular subversion of New Testament Christianity the "Baal of happiness." It is hell's zealous agent. Each book of the New Testament does battle against it. In the Book of Revelation the Laodicean church had become its victim.

In this chapter we will find that the Baal of happiness had hold of "Rocky" too.

The pertinent scriptures are the Gospel of Mark and 1 and 2 Peter.

— 7 —

THE BAAL OF HAPPINESS

I have accumulated names the way a ship collects barnacles. "Rocky" is one of them. That's what you can call me.

My sharp disappointment over what increasingly looks like a failed venture has left me confused and uncertain about the future. My brother is "up to his neck" in this thing also. A few minutes ago I received a shock that intensified my alarm. If you can spare time, please hear my story. I have heard about some of your prayers and aspirations. I think you will appreciate my quandary and will probably take my side.

THE INVESTMENT

Almost two years ago, my brother and I signed on to support a most promising fellow who calls himself the *Son of Man*. I thought that perhaps he might be the Messiah. For years, many Jews have interpreted the "one like unto a son of man" spoken of by Daniel to be the Messiah—a heavenly ruler sent by God. He would destroy the powers of evil and inaugurate the kingdom of God. So when the *Son of Man* showed up and called me to follow him, I was confident my big break had come. My life—and that of my extended family—was about to improve greatly. I shelved my regular day job and threw everything into the venture. Yes, I "bet the bank" as you say.

However, in recent weeks, disturbing reasons for alarm have been popping up. It looks more and more as though I might have shown very poor judgment that day along the shore of Galilee. Some people already accuse me of having foolishly lurched into things.

If my risky venture goes bankrupt, I suppose I can pick up my old trade. But the disappointment would never leave me—my hopes have soared so high. Can you imagine my embarrassment? For starters, what would I tell my wife who has been patient through it all? I told her prospects for success were 100 percent favorable. What would I tell my aged father, who held the nets and shook his head when my brother and I left the boats behind? Even worse, what will I tell my mother-in-law? I have spent years trying to convince her that I am good enough for her daughter. What if I have to return home with my "tail between my legs"?

How will I explain things to the other fishermen in my village? On the day we left, they called out, "There goes ol' Rocky, chasing another one of his dreams." If I crawl back home, they will say, "Well, Rocky, you should have known your place and stayed in it. You got too big for your britches."

PLACE

Speaking of "place," I should explain that I am a strictly observant Jew. We live under the domination of the Romans and are ruled by their appointed governors called tetrarchs. Except for one period of independence, for six hundred years our land has been ruled by other nations—Babylonians, Persians, Greeks, and Romans.

Have you heard that Palestine has many poor people? I am one of them. There are two kinds of poor people: "working poor" and "begging poor." The working poor consist of merchants, artisans, farmers, and fishermen. As fishermen, my father, brother, and I were completely dependent on our catch and the market. We didn't have the rich gentry's luxury of leisure time.

But the working poor do have a measure of self-sufficiency. We also enjoy a measure of honor and respect. Beneath us are the begging poor—total strangers to honor and respect. They are destitute of all means of support, such as a farm, a trade, family, and social ties. Finding their daily bread is a struggle. Many of them wander from place to place. Many of them were once working poor. But because of heavy taxation, illness, or other misfortune, they lost their meager resources and dropped into the ranks of the begging poor. Most of the working poor face that threat; the wolf is always at our door. Except for our meager family resources, we have no safety net.

Everyone—including the working poor—is under a sacred obligation to give alms to the begging poor. We expect God to bless us in return.

I mentioned taxes. They seem to dominate our lives. We pay a fee to fish the Sea of Galilee—in a specific area. We pay a tax to the toll collectors before we can take our catch to market. When we sell our catch, it is taxed. On top of all that, each year the tax collector comes around for more taxes. Even if we catch a boatload of fish, after we pay tolls and taxes not much is left. Business and family must still be supported. I haven't even mentioned what we must give to the temple.

Are you surprised that I would look for opportunities to improve my situation?

MAPS

I told you that I am a devoutly observant Jew. We Jews live by what might be called maps of purity. We received them over the years from the elders of our faith. Although there is debate among us about where some people and things fit, our purity maps structure our society and shape our obedience to the whole Law, or Way of the Lord. They show us the status of our standing before God. Adherence yields purity; violation surrenders purity. We have "a place for everything and everything has its place." Among us, holiness—which for us means "wholeness"—is measured by degrees. Some people are more "whole" (holy) than others. One's degree of holiness is decided by one's assigned position in our religious and cultural structure. Priests are more holy than Levites, and born Israelites are more holy than converts. The holiness of people and places is rated according to their proximity to the Jerusalem temple. As a place, the land of Israel is more holy than any other land.

Our number of maps might surprise you. In addition to maps of *places*, there are maps of *persons*. They meticulously classify the people of Israel. We have maps of *time*—Sabbath, Feast of Passover, and Day of Atonement. Maps of the *body* regulate what enters and exits. Maps also identify the *outside* boundaries we must not cross. *Internal* boundaries are defined. Dead Israelites, and morally and bodily unclean Israelites, form internal boundaries. Boundaries let us know who is in the covenant community and who is out.

Of course, I assumed the *Son of Man* shared our allegiance to the maps. Almost everyone had heard how John the Baptist had placed his stamp of approval on him—even said his own honor should decrease and the *Son of Man*'s honor would increase. No pious Jew in our village would have questioned that endorsement.

HOW THE WORLD OPERATES

Not only am I a devout Jew, but my fellow Jews and I are also shaped by some of the social arrangements that shape the larger Roman and Greek culture. Deeply embedded in all our social relationships is what we call the patron-client system. It is a social arrangement based on *inequality* and *reciprocity* between two or more people. A patron is someone who has things a client needs. These might be land, military leadership, food, or an appointment to political office. A patron gives resources to one or more clients under carefully defined conditions. A client, on the other hand, has something the patron needs. He can give loyal service and show honor to his patron. So the system is strictly reciprocal and balanced between benefits given and loyalty returned. Patrons and clients benefit. Often go-betweens, called brokers, help make arrangements between potential patrons and potential clients. We are barely conscious of how far the patron-client system reaches into our lives. It's just the way our world works.

One might be a patron in one setting and a client in another. The emperor is the chief patron of the empire. His treasure of dispensable resources surpasses all other patrons—except the gods to whom he is a client and from whom he receives benefactions. The role reversal plays out all the way down the line. Even the working poor can be patrons to the begging poor; they can give alms. God will reciprocate on behalf of the begging poor. He will heap benefits upon givers of alms.

Meanwhile, clients work to climb the ladder of benefactions by showing loyalty and honor.

Wealth is assessed according to the measure of one's patronage and the status or honor that accrues to it. Money is not the primary standard. With increased patronage come increased honor and power. Honor, wealth, and power are inseparable. Patrons work to increase all three. With them comes the greatest prize of all—happiness. A patron's wealth should be expressed through consumption and display. This can be done in banquets, fine clothes, weapons, or houses. Those who receive the benefits of expressed wealth must be clients, who can return the favor by showing honor and pledging loyal service.

An important exception to this arrangement operates within close family relationships. Here, giving is mostly one-sided, altruistic. Gifts are given in the absence of stated requirements for return in kind.

Almost unquestioned is the belief that happiness is one of life's most important pursuits. We milk the patron-client system for all it's worth. With happiness comes security. That's especially critical for the working poor, like me, who might easily fall into the ranks of the begging poor.

A smart man is always seeking a good—or even better—patron. The more a patron has to offer, the better off a willing and able client will be.

MY PATRON

I have told you this so that you can see why the *Son of Man* was so attractive to me—even compelling.

I thought I had found the perfect patron. Most people didn't see it, but I did. I listened carefully to reports of what John the Baptist said about him—more powerful than John himself, not worthy to touch the feet of the *Son of Man*, and John the forerunner of the Messiah. I am no religious scholar, but I knew the Messiah would deliver Israel from foreign control. Political sovereignty would be restored. The Anointed One would establish the kingdom of God by imposing the reign of justice upon the world's power structures.

Who wouldn't want to be the client of a patron like that—especially if you could be one of the Kingdom's charter members? On the day when the *Son of Man* showed up and invited us to sign on, we couldn't store our fishnets fast enough. "Just give us a few moments, Sir." With good-byes said all around, my brother and I took the plunge.

Do you understand what it would mean to be the Messiah's client? We expected him to expel the Romans and rule over God's universal kingdom. His benefits—status, power, abundance—would flow to loyal clients. I intended to be positioned as close to this patron as possible. Just imagining the benefits made me dizzy.

Happiness, here I come!

Almost immediately the *Son of Man* began to do things that seemed to confirm my hopes. He preached that God was inaugurating the kingdom of God through him. To prove it, he demonstrated his authority by performing miracles and forgiving sins. For starters, in the synagogue he cast a demon out of a possessed man. He touched a leper and healed him. A paralyzed man was not only healed but also forgiven of his sins. A young maiden who had died was restored to life.

Forces of nature yielded to him. One evening, as we were facing death on the raging sea, he spoke forcefully and calmed the storm. Even a whole force of demons obeyed him when he commanded them to leave a poor, abandoned man living in a cemetery.

Against a patron like the *Son of Man*, the Romans wouldn't stand a chance.

SIGNS OF TROUBLE

However, despite the miracles and the preaching, I saw disturbing signs. The *Son of Man* didn't act much like a patron. Shortly after I signed on, we went into the town of Capernaum, where he healed my mother-in-law, who was sick with a fever. Word spread quickly. Almost the whole town came running. People began bringing their sick and demon-possessed friends and family members to the *Son of Man* for healing. He astonished everyone by casting out demons and commanding them to be quiet.

I am working poor, but I know how patrons build their power bases. Just such an opportunity had been placed before the *Son of Man*. He had bestowed benefactions on many people. Now all of them were indebted to him. Had he recognized his opportunity, he would have remained in place and continued to bestow benefactions. He would have multiplied his number of clients and multiplied his power. His power would have been recognized as wealth, which he could have begun to display (to my benefit also, I might add). That is the way you establish power and wealth in our culture.

He was in the perfect place to accomplish all of this. Capernaum is strategically located on a major road that leads from Damascus to Galilee. It carries military, commercial, and human traffic that stops in town for food and rest. A steady stream of potential clients would have poured in. Capernaum also has a stately synagogue that could have served as the *Son of Man's* religious base. Added to Jesus being my patron, I could have been his chief broker, a go-between to connect Jesus and his growing list of clients. It would be win-win in every direction.

None of this happened. Instead, long before daybreak the next day, the *Son of Man* pulled up stakes and went off to a lonely place to pray. I and some others tracked him down and tried to explain the rules of patronage. He seemed not to comprehend—wasn't even interested. Instead of returning to base, he squandered his good start by taking off for other villages, where he had to start all over!

As an observant Jew, I also was disturbed over how the *Son of Man* disregarded our purity maps. He seemed to be guided by an understanding of purity that didn't require them. He ignored the *purity map of people* who should be avoided. He touched a leper, a menstruating woman, and even called Levi—a collector of Roman taxes—to be an intimate follower.

The *Son of Man* transgressed the *map of the body* by disregarding Jewish dietary restrictions. He didn't ritually wash before eating and did not require his disciples to do so, either. One day he even applied his own spittle to the eyes of a blind man.

Our *map of time* by which we organize our lives was also infringed upon. He seemed to delight in healing on the Sabbath. He permitted us to pluck grain on the Sabbath. He even claimed to be Lord of the Sabbath. All in all, he went around acting as though God's grace is free and unpredictable.

Before long, he ran afoul of the Pharisees. They observed and concluded that far from being the Holy One of God, the devil had sent the *Son of Man*.

I had serious misgiving as well, but my doubts were checked by counter evidence. John the Baptist had said that whereas he had baptized with water, the *Son of Man* would baptize with the Holy Spirit. A sinner could not do that. During the *Son of Man's* baptism, God himself had borne witness to his holiness and purity. After the *Son of Man's* temptation by the devil, God sent angels to minister to him. This proved God's favor toward him. The Holy Spirit had been with the *Son of Man* the whole time he was in the wilderness.

Despite my doubts, that was enough to continue as his client.

THE CRISIS

By and large, things were moving along quite well. The adoring crowds were increasing. My brother and I were selected as members of the traveling team—and me to the inner circle. One day he gave us power over unclean spirits and sent us out in pairs to preach in the towns and villages. To the crowds' delight, the *Son of Man* was holding his own against the Pharisees.

Happily, my hopes about his patronage seemed to be stabilizing.

Then it happened. Everything collapsed. Adjustments became impossible. The *Son of Man* began saying things that unmistakably contradicted the meaning of "Messiah." If what he was saying about himself was true, he could never be a patron—certainly not the Messiah. My hope of being his client would perish as well.

Yesterday, as we were traveling to the villages in the vicinity of Caesarea Philippi, the *Son of Man* asked us, "Who do you guys think I am?" That question was not difficult to answer. Being one who usually spoke first, I answered, "You are the Messiah we have expected for so long." Naturally, I was quite pleased with myself. My brother nodded his approval.

As I was bathing in satisfaction, the *Son of Man* shattered everything I had believed about him. He told us that he was on course to suffer many things at the hands of his enemies. He would be rejected by our religious leaders—the very ones who should be his allies in establishing God's kingdom. He compounded our dismay by saying that our religious leaders would cooperate with the Romans to crucify him. More contradictory words could not have been spoken. A powerless and dead Messiah? A defenseless Messiah crucified by his enemies? Absolutely nothing in our Jewish expectations made place for that. You might as well expect waterless rain.

I immediately saw the consequences of what the *Son of Man* had just said. We Jews have no place at all for a suffering Messiah. What a contradiction! A dead Messiah would be no patron at all—for Israel or for me. Suffering and being killed on a cross by the Romans would completely eliminate all prospects for honor and power. Discrediting shame would be the *Son of Man*'s portion—and ours. All our political hopes would perish.

Unless things could be reversed quickly, unless the *Son of Man* could be brought to his senses, my investment in his patronage would go belly-up. Good-bye, happiness.

REBUKES

Being a person of decisive action, I discreetly took the *Son of Man* aside and scolded him—something completely out of character for clients. But emergency situations require bold action.

You might have expected his response to be as discreet as my counsel. Not so. Before all the disciples, the *Son of Man* looked directly at me and said: "You are of the devil, one of his allies. Get behind me. Your ambitions and desires are just like his. They certainly didn't come from God."

I was completely dumbstruck—paralyzed by shame. My chief patron had just called me Lucifer. My failure to understand him, he said, and my attempt to tell him how to be the Messiah prompted his rebuke. Imagine! The *Son of Man* had associated me with his chief enemy—the Tempter. I was his agent, seeking to turn the *Son of Man* away from his mission.

While I stood looking like a fool, the *Son of Man* made matters worse. He called us to himself, and said: "Let's get this straight. If you want to become my disciples, you will have to do it on my terms, not yours. Make no mistake; you will have to take up a cross just like I will, and all of you know what a cross involves."

Not only must my expectations about his patronage die, but so must my expectations about being his client. None of us standing there needed to be told what it meant for Roman soldiers to show up in a village, seize an accused man, place a crossbeam upon his shoulders, and lead him away to crucifix-ion. He wouldn't be coming back.

Perhaps you can understand that we could not compre-hend what the *Son of Man* was saying. It struck us as nonsense. He had just turned the meaning of patron and client upside down. Rather than accumulating the world's honor, power, and wealth, the *Son of Man* would reject it all. Something much greater, more eternal, would be his goal. Given that redefini-tion, "client" would change its meaning too.

At that moment, the magnitude of the error of leaving home tumbled in upon me. What was I to do? Home was about forty miles away. I could be there in a few days.

If I were to remain with the *Son of Man, everything* would have to change. He would be free to redefine my expectations of him, to reconstruct my self-understanding, and to alter all my hopes. Nothing—including happiness—would ever be the same.

YOUR COUNSEL, PLEASE

After a sleepless night filled with anguished reflection, I must make a decision—leave or stay.

Now that you understand my crisis, "What should I do—go home or remain with this non-patron? What would you do?"

Quick, he's leaving—again.

Getting Ready to Hear
(Chapter 8)

The New Testament church was tempted to plant the Baal Conspiracy deep in its soil. The Roman Empire offered a ready pattern for organizing political and social institutions. The model relied on impressive social, political, and military power. Philosophers and statesmen supplied the wisdom needed for establishing and maintaining civil and domestic institutions. Roman power and careful social stratification could catalog impressive achievements.

But the apostle Paul stoutly rejected the Roman way as a model for preaching the gospel and establishing the Church. He asked the Corinthian Christians, "Where is the wise man? . . . Where is the debater of this age? Has not God made foolish the wisdom of the world? For since, in the wisdom of God, the world did not know God through wisdom, it pleased God through the folly of what we preach to save those who believe. . . . For the foolishness of God is wiser than men, and the weakness of God is stronger than men" (1 Cor. 1:20-25, RSV). Paul wanted the Corinthians' faith to rest in the power of God, not in the wisdom of men (see 2:5).

The gospel and the Church's life derive from an order of reality about which the unredeemed world knows nothing. Clearly, the gospel cannot be rightly proclaimed and the Church rightly expressed if Christians try to root them in this world's values. Yet, that is exactly the threat Paul confronted in the Corinthian church. Some of its members were trying to use the wisdom and power of the old fallen order to understand and live the new creation.

One major error was associated with the Lord's Supper and the common meal that usually preceded it. It cropped up after Paul left the city. He had arrived in AD 50 during his second missionary journey (Acts 18:1-18). He established the church and remained as its pastor for about eighteen months. Leaving Corinth, Paul sailed east to Ephesus on his way to Syria (Antioch). While in Ephesus he wrote letters to the Corinthians, one of which we call 1 Corinthians.

Some people were trying to organize the Lord's Supper according to Greco-Roman social stratification and clout. They were injecting into the Eucharist the very power and hierarchy Jesus rejected during the first Eucharist.

Had the error succeeded—and had it spread to the other Gentile churches—the gospel of Jesus Christ would have been stillborn in the Greco-Roman world. In 1 Corinthians Paul confronts the threat head-on. One of the perpetrators tells the story.

The Baal of power we encounter in this chapter is no respecter of eras, doctrines, persons, or denominations. Allowed to thrive, it will mock the gospel of Jesus Christ and subvert the Church's life and character. Church history bears witness.

The pertinent scriptures are Acts 18:1-18; 1 Cor. 1:18—2:8; 11:17-34.

8

THE BAAL OF POWER IN THE CHURCH

Welcome to Corinth, my friend. Thanks for coming. I hope you can help resolve a conflict.

Let's step into the shade and away from this scorching sun. By the puzzled look on your face I see that you are wondering, "Why are they loading that cargo ship onto the wheeled cart?" I will explain.

Yesterday the ship arrived here at Lechaion. It was carrying wine, olive oil, fish sauce, and other goods. The limestone-paved path you see rising to the crest of the hill runs southeastward for four miles across the Isthmus of Corinth. It terminates at the port of Cenchreae in the Saronic Gulf. We call the tracks and path the "haul across." Yes, they are quite old. Periander, ruler of Corinth about six hundred years ago, built them. The ship now being placed on the cart will be pulled along the tracks to Cenchreae, reloaded, and then sent on its way East. Next, a ship coming from the East will be loaded and wheeled to Lechaeum, where it will continue westward—perhaps to Italy.

Larger ships unload their cargo and remain in port. We wheel their cargo across the Isthmus and load it onto other ships. Pulling ships and cargo along the "haul across" occurs all day, seven days a week, as weather and festivals permit. As you can see, the "haul across" lets ships avoid a lengthy journey around the southern end of Greece.

The two seaports and the "haul across" are cash cows for Corinth. The city collects a toll for each ship and cargo. Revenue generated by the ports, profits from trade that moves north and south, and the prized Corinthian bronze, textiles, and pottery the city exports account for Corinth's economic success.

As everyone knows, Corinth is well known for its money and love of parties. Matching that are its lax sexual boundaries and large athletic spectacles. You might already know that in the spring of every second year we recognize our debt to the sea by celebrating the Isthmian Games in honor of Poseidon—god of the sea.

As you might expect, while ships are docked in the seaports awaiting their turns at the "haul across," their crews dive into the city where they visit Corinth's famous prostitutes and crowd its taverns. They buy clothing and equipment, visit the theater and the city's temples—including the temple of Aphrodite on the Acrocorinth. Look to the southwest. The Acrocorinth is the limestone mountain you see in the distance.

Given Corinth's diversity of human traffic and residents, it easily mixes all kinds of religious beliefs and practices. With all the hustle and bustle, the city never sleeps.

Remember that our city is young by Greek standards. The Romans destroyed the old Greek city about two hundred years ago. About one hundred years later, Julius Caesar rebuilt it as a colony for military veterans. Placing veterans here took them out of Italy where they might cause the emperor trouble. They stimulated the city's economy and promoted Roman culture in a Greek world. Corinth's relatively recent beginning means we don't have landed and aristocratic families who exercise elite privileges. The city is largely populated by freed Roman slaves, Greeks, and Jews.

All of this makes upward social mobility more possible than in most Greek and Roman cities. I should know because I have profited quiet well from the opportunities. Like many other well-to-do Corinthians, I arrived years ago as a freed and ambitious slave. The city was tailor-made for an enterprising man, and I took full advantage. I now own five of those wheeled cradles that carry the ships. I employ two crews to make arrangements with ship captains. My slaves pull the carts from port to port. My son and I do a little exporting on the side. Without boasting, I must admit that the business has turned this freed slave into a fairly wealthy man. I am now well placed in Corinthian society. My home is in a preferred part of the city. Its architecture and imported furnishings bear testimony to my affluence and social standing. Although I arrived in this city as a nobody, my family has become a fixture in the city's better social circles.

A little more than two years ago a most remarkable thing happened, and that quite unexpectedly. A friend named Titius Justus introduced me to a Jew named Paul who, along with his partner Timothy, had recently arrived from Athens. I must say that physically, Paul was a most unimpressive figure. He seemed to be bothered by some sort of illness I couldn't figure out. He was a preacher who came to the city declaring a message about Jesus of Nazareth—a Jewish preacher whom the Romans had crucified in Jerusalem some years before. Paul said this Jesus was the Messiah, the Christ, whom God had promised to the Jews. He declared that even though Jesus had been crucified, three days later God raised him from the dead, confirming him as the Messiah and Redeemer. Paul preached that salvation through the name of Jesus was now available to everyone. They wouldn't even have to become Jewish proselytes. Paul preached that Christ could free us from our fear of hostile heavenly powers and from our fear of death. He would make us children of God. All that struck me like a thunderbolt of good news.

To support himself, Paul teamed up with two other Christians—Aquila and his wife, Priscilla—to make and sell leather goods. They, too, were Jews recently arrived from Rome. Emperor Claudius (AD 41-54) had required Jews to leave Rome. So Aquila and Priscilla migrated to Corinth.

Paul's attempts to persuade Corinthian Jews to embrace Jesus as Messiah failed. Most Jews in the synagogue where Paul spoke reviled his message. One exception was Crispus, president of the synagogue, who believed. Unable to gain a hearing, Paul changed his strategy and began preaching the good news of Jesus to the Gentiles. My friend Titius received Paul's message, confessed faith in the risen Christ, and offered his house as a place for people to hear Paul preach. Titius is what the Jews call a God-fearer—a Gentile who worships the God of the Jews. He attended synagogue services, participated in some of the ceremonial requirements, and practiced the morality the Jews teach. But he had not been circumcised and so had not become a complete convert.

More Gentile Corinthians received the good news. They rejoiced to learn that through Jesus' crucifixion and resurrection, God acted to free them from bondage to their pagan ways. Good News! No matter our past or social position, we could become new people in Christ and full members of God's family.

As people responded, the church in Titius's house grew. Before long, his house was not big enough. More house assemblies were added. One house assembly meets in nearby Cenchreae. A female Christian named Phoebe is one of its leaders.

Because of the way Paul preached, anyone—including slaves and women—who heard and received the gospel was then baptized and became a member of the church. Now the church in Corinth mirrors much of Corinth's population. Paul insisted that the gospel of Christ negates all distinctions of privilege between Jews and Greeks, slaves and freedmen, male and female. I agree with him up to a point. I'll tell you more in a moment about the dispute between Paul and me. I think you will take my side.

A few members of the church are among the city's powerful people—a sprinkling of wealthy folk and civil officials such as Erastus the city's treasurer. Some of us are considered wise by the standards of Corinthian culture. Only a couple members can claim elite birth. Some are slaves, some are women, and most come from what we might call the working class. Some members are freedmen artisans. Only a few can read and write. Some of our more influential members are Chloe, Stephanas, Fortunatus, and Achaicus. Not long ago, most of us were steeped in Corinth's pagan ways. Paul pegs us correctly by reminding us that by society's standards not many of us would count as wise, not many as politically powerful, and certainly not many as highborn.

Paul stayed in our city for eighteen months. While here, he made new converts and taught us. As the church grew, opposition from some of the Jews accelerated. The Jewish leaders hauled Paul before Gallio, proconsul of the province of Achaia. They accused him of convincing Jews to worship God in a way contrary to the Law of Moses. Gallio would not bog down the Roman justice system in what he thought was just a religious dispute. He told them to settle their argument among themselves. And settle it they did; they turned upon Sosthenes, the new president of the synagogue, and beat him in Gallio's presence.

A few months later, Paul and some of his associates—including Priscilla and Aquila—sailed from Cenchreae. Syria was his destination. But Ephesus was his first stop.

After Paul left, problems cropped up in the church. He sent a letter meant to resolve the problems. He warned us not to mingle with those who claim to be Christians but who continue to be sexually immoral or greedy. The same applies to so-called Christians who go on worshipping idols, slandering others, stealing, and getting drunk. Paul said we should not even eat with people who tarnish the name of Christ.

The letter did not end the church's troubles. Problems multiplied until the church looked like a stew of conflicts. Chloe, one of our leaders, sent representatives to Paul to get help and to report on the church's troubles. We had questions about sexual relations between husbands and wives, about whether or not young people should get married, and whether Christian slaves should insist on being set free. A big dispute developed over whether Christians should buy and eat meat sacrificed to idols in pagan temples. Another conflict erupted over how to rank spiritual gifts. That led to a lot of bragging by some who think they are at the top of the scale. Other members are teaching that the Lord has already returned. This has left some of the newer Christians deeply confused.

Before Paul had time to address this list of problems, Stephanas, Fortunatus, and Achaicus sailed to Ephesus to tell Paul about the worsening situation. Paul quickly fired off a long letter that tackled all the problems one by one. Timothy brought Paul's letter to us and then stuck around for a few weeks to catch our response. What he saw was not encouraging. Much of what Paul had written was either misunderstood or ignored. Some members are now challenging Paul's authority as an apostle.

Yesterday Timothy set sail for Ephesus where in a few weeks he will make his grim report to Paul. I can already see him fuming (he does have a temper). Given the importance Paul attaches to our church, I expect that he will promptly set sail for Corinth and try to solve the problems in person. If the weather continues to be favorable, a couple of months from now I expect to hear that Paul has landed at Cenchreae. His coming will be painful; he will be "in our faces."

When he arrives, I will be one of his chief targets. That is why I asked you to come before Paul gets here. I have postponed telling you about my conflict with Paul until now. A few other church members strongly support my side. Paul laid out his position in the letter Timothy brought. He is no doubt an authority on many things, but in this instance he is culturally naïve. Some of us have noticed that Paul's education sometimes causes him to ignore hard-nosed social reality.

Let me lay the conflict before you. Given your reputation for common sense, you will see that Paul is dead wrong.

Our dispute involves the Eucharist—the Lord's Supper. I agree that the good news of Jesus Christ is meant for everyone without respect for gender or social status. Salvation is meant for slaves as much as for the nobility. But Paul has taken his rejection of social distinctions and power structures entirely too far. He shows all the signs of your typical religious zealot who drives a good thing into the ground. Paul has no comprehension of the role of power in an orderly society and doesn't appreciate what culture contributes to the church.

What he advocates for the church in the name of Jesus—a careless abuse of Jesus so far as I am concerned—would bring down upon our heads the ridicule and wrath of Roman society. There are respected age-old social norms that exist for good reason; they also must function in the church. Otherwise, chaos will follow.

Are you with me so far?

As I mentioned, we worship in the homes of the few members who have large houses. The quarters where Aquila and Priscilla live provide one meeting place. No house in Corinth is large enough to place all the Christians who meet there in one room.

Customarily, when well-to-do Corinthian citizens host banquets in their homes, they put their guests in various rooms. The rule for distributing guests is clearly understood. Guests who have the highest social status by virtue of their power, wealth, or wisdom sit in the best parts of the house. In descending order of importance, other guests sit in lesser rooms. Those nearer the bottom of the scale go to the atrium.

The same rule applies to food. The guests who occupy the highest social level eat the best foods. Guests in the atrium get the lowest quality. The choice guests might eat oysters, mushrooms, and turtledoves. The people in the atrium might eat mussels, hog fungus, and magpies. The choice guests will receive their food first. Someone always grumbles about where he has been seated.

That is the arrangement we use in the church for the love feast that precedes the Lord's Supper. It stands to reason, doesn't it, that we would use our standard cultural pattern when trying to organize meals in houses? The well-to-do church members bring the kind of food they want, and the poorer members bring what they can afford. The well-to-do members proceed to eat before the poorer members begin. Admittedly, sometimes the better-off members drink too much of the wine they bring in their flasks. But that often happens at Corinthian banquets.

Had it not been for some disgruntled people in the church who complained about their assigned places, the dispute with Paul would not have happened. For a person who insists on the insignificance of seasons, days, and diets, as Paul does, his fussing about where people sit seems to be a waste of time. What he labels divisive "factions" are nothing more than long-standing social distinctions all church members should respect.

We use the same social arrangement for the Eucharist—the Lord's Supper. Members seated in the atrium are served last.

You can see that these distinctions don't interfere with recognizing as Christians all those who partake of the Lord's Supper. Where they sit makes no difference. The arrangement just recognizes natural and achieved differences in power, influence, and ability. Everyone—Paul included—should respect this.

Our pattern for placing church members should remain. Recognizing power and influence in the church is inevitable. Acting otherwise is naïve and self-deceptive.

Paul is bent out of shape over our arrangement—downright angry. I will relay what he says. You can judge.

Paul says our arrangement attacks the foundation of the Church. He says it subverts the gospel of Jesus Christ. Going completely overboard, Paul says that when we arrange people as we do, we aren't even eating the Lord's Supper. Instead, we are practicing a farce. He says we don't even understand the Lord's Supper, the church, or the gospel. Using the Roman seating arrangement for the love feast and the Lord's Supper expresses contempt for the Church of God. Paul claims that we are piling humiliation upon the poor—upon Christ's sisters and brothers. He says we are eating and drinking unworthily; we don't even know the meaning of the Body of Christ.

According to Paul, in the original Lord's Supper Jesus rejected the Roman hierarchy of power and privilege as the norm for his disciples' life together. As the disciples scratched for position, Jesus tied a towel around his waist, took a basin of water, and began to wash their feet. He freely forfeited his own exalted status as Lord and Master. Jesus told the shocked disciples that he was among them not as a powerful lord exercising his privileges but as one performing the lowly service of a servant.

Paul claims that Jesus turned the world of power and position upside down.

The self-emptying Christ demonstrated, Paul insists, should be the foundation and model for the Church. Paul wants to scrub from the Church the Roman pattern of privilege and power. Otherwise, he insists, we will not understand the kingdom of God.

Now, doesn't all that strike you as abstract and impractical nonsense?

Paul claims that if we retain the structure I am promoting, it will mean we did not correctly hear the gospel he came preaching. He says he told us plainly from the beginning that God did not use this world's pattern of power and wisdom to reveal his grace. Instead, he chose what the world calls foolish and weak to manifest his wisdom and power. In the cross, Paul says, God rejected all boasting based on social clout, moral achievement, and religious privilege. He sternly tells us that the cross of Christ negates the privileges we have been mixing into the Eucharist. In the Lord's Supper, Paul claims, we all drink equally of one Spirit and one grace—the very thing our classifications threaten.

"You need not tell me," Paul seems to shout, "that life in Christ cuts across the structures Roman culture considers normal." Roman society will call his rejection of power and privilege foolish. But what is at stake, he claims, is the very character and supremacy of the kingdom of God. Paul insists we must decide whether we believe the future belongs to Rome or to the kingdom of God. That is a choice I don't think we have to make.

I think you can see how impractical and unsustainable Paul's argument is. Although sincere, he is an idealistic dreamer. When the Lord returns, Paul can have his way. Until then, common sense must rule.

You can see that if Paul arrives, his airy dreams will have no chance against my hard-nosed realism.

Agreed?

Getting Ready to Hear

(Chapter 9)

The Book of Hebrews records some of the most assuring and yet impenetrable words of the New Testament: "For because he himself has suffered and been tempted, he is able to help those who are tempted. . . . in every respect [he] has been tempted as we are, yet without sin" (Heb. 2:18; 4:15, RSV).

We have entered the region of divine condescension (see Phil. 2:5-11) and cannot fully comprehend the meaning of God's Son being tempted. We bow in wondrous awe as he "[learns] obedience through what he [suffers]" (Heb. 5:8, RSV).

After Jesus' baptism, led by the Holy Spirit, he entered the wilderness. There he fasted for a long time. Matthew, Mark, and Luke say he was tempted by Satan (Matt. 4:1-2; Mark 1:12-13; Luke 4:1-4). One look at the barren land that rises to the mountains west of the Jordan is enough to provoke shudders when considering Jesus being tested there.

Some scholars say that Jesus is being tempted in the wilderness even as ancient Israel was tempted in the wilderness, except that Israel failed the test (Deut. 6-8). Jesus is tested as the unique Son of God. He relies upon the Holy Spirit and the Word of God—resources available to all Jesus' disciples.

By tempting Jesus, the Chief Conspirator made his most astonishing move. He tried to subvert Jesus' obedience to his Father without inviting outright rebellion. True to the nature of the Baal Conspiracy, the only thing Satan sought to achieve was for Jesus to distort his trust in the Father. That alone would have been enough to abort Jesus' mission. Satan attacked from three directions (physical needs, the lure of earthly power, and testing God). He continues to use these tactics when trying to get Christians to adopt a twisted understanding of faith.

Why was Jesus tempted? Christians affirm that Christ "is truly God and truly man." He is complete in his deity and humanity (the Creed of Chalcedon, AD 451). Among other things, this means that our Lord radically identified with us, including our being tempted. Apart from being "tempted as we are" (Heb. 4:15, RSV), Jesus could not have fully represented us before the Father. He would have skirted the zone of danger where we are most vulnerable. Jesus did not seek a privileged exemption from temptation. Instead, "although he was a Son, he learned obedience" through his own testing—beginning in the wilderness (5:8). He put the "omnis" on hold (omnipotence, omnipresence, etc.) and never pushed the "God button" for escape. Only then could he "[become] the author of eternal salvation" (v. 9, NKJV).

The Incarnation was real.

The pertinent scriptures are Deut. 6:13-19; Ps. 91:11-12; Matt. 4:1-11; Mark 1:12-13; Luke 4:1-13; Heb. 2:10-18; 4:15; 5:7-8.

9

THE CHALLENGE

For millennia, I have *longed* for this day. For millennia, I have *dreaded* this day. Now it is here. I have longed to finish my work begun long ago in that lush garden, so unlike this scorching wilderness. Since then I've known a decisive struggle was inevitable. Now the final battle will begin—eyeball to eyeball. My Conspiracy will now snare its most coveted prize.

I dread the magnitude of my opponent and the possibility of failure. I expect he will be frightful to behold.

But I will not fail. Millennia of preparation and millions of conquests have sharpened my ability to deceive. My plan of attack has been tested and proven effective. There is no reason to change now.

THE SENDER

The *Sender* has already made a foolish blunder that gives me the upper hand. Can you believe it? He has carelessly clothed his *Christos** in the vulnerability of human flesh, complete with its strengths and weaknesses, desires and emotions. Why should I care? The blunder has made me stronger. I am an experienced master at exploiting human weaknesses. History is littered by the debris of my successes.

---

*Christos is the Greek word for "the Anointed One," the Messiah

You would think the *Sender* would have profited from his first humiliating failure to achieve loving obedience in humans. The world just isn't tailored for faithful worship and love. I proudly engineered the *Sender*'s failure in the Garden of Eden. I will do it again in this godforsaken wilderness.

THE *CHRISTOS*

I admit I have never faced a foe like the *Christos*. But I am confident about the outcome. He has carelessly emptied himself of all his divine privileges. Now he is vulnerability personified. All I have to do is stick with the game plan. His being a rustic Galilean, the religious leaders in Jerusalem will ridicule him as their cultural inferior—a "country cousin come to town." I will exploit his social inferiority.

Why is the *Christos* here? Signals about his coming have been received from the prophets. They have called him Immanuel as a promise that the *Sender* will not forsake his people. They have named him "Redeemer," expecting him to ransom those who have fallen under my sway. The prophets say the *Christos* will bind up the brokenhearted and cure bleeding souls. He is expected to tear down the gates of hell and break the iron fetters I have so skillfully crafted. Many say he will scatter the proud and put down the mighty from their thrones. They expect him to exalt those of low degree and fill the hungry with good things.

Such expectations reveal the massive threat the *Christos* presents to the admirable kingdoms I have built. If he were to succeed, he would lay a foundation for undoing all I have accomplished since the days of Adam. The prophets say he is bent on releasing the creation from its bondage and restoring to the *Sender* all things in heaven and earth. He intends to change slaves into children of God and clothe them with unspeakable blessings and joy. The *Christos* plans to call these people his "Church," even his "Body." The *Sender* will use Holy Love instead of force to accomplish his goals. How stupid! My contempt for his plan is ancient and incorrigible.

The *Sender* has heard the creation groaning under the oppression I have imposed. Through the *Christos,* the *Sender* intends to create a new heaven and a new earth where even he can freely dwell.

If the *Christos* were to succeed, he would then be seated at the *Sender's* right hand. He would be elevated above all rulers, authorities, and kingdoms. He would reign as head over all things throughout eternity.

Were the *Christos* to fulfill the *Sender's* plans, my days would be numbered. All my allies and I would be judged and publically humiliated before the nations. We would be stripped of all our power and consigned to hell forever—divinely imposed carnage!

This must not happen. The *Christos* must be stopped before the wreckage occurs. Let the battle begin!

THE CHALLENGE

Is that him I see coming? It can't be. Nothing about him is impressive. Obviously fatigued, he is lamentable to behold. He looks like a lamb readied for slaughter. What was the *Sender* thinking by pitting such comical weakness against me? My point of attack will be the glaring vulnerability of this *Christos.*

Still, I must be on my guard. I puzzle over one thing—why would the *Sender* make the same mistake twice? Given all he wants to accomplish, why not shield the *Christos* against my blows? Why permit him to be assailed and tested? Why the risk of a second failure?

Does the *Sender* somehow intend to bind himself to his creation? Doesn't he realize once the battle is joined there will be no turning back? At any rate, that is his problem. My task and opportunity are clear: the *Christos* must become my ally, even if unwittingly. A wedge must be driven between the *Sender* and the *Christos*. Human history *and* my own fate hang in the balance.

A few weeks ago, when John the Baptist baptized the *Christos* in the Jordan River, the Holy Spirit descended upon him. The *Sender* announced, "You are my Son. You are my chosen One. I am well pleased with you." That announcement will be my point of attack; I'll subvert the *Christos*'s trust in the *Sender*.

I will not foolishly try to convince the *Christos* that he is not the Son of God or try to provoke an open rupture. I will be much more subtle. I will convince the *Christos* to distort his relationship with the *Sender* by embracing a deceptive and distorted understanding of faith. His exhaustion is poised for exploitation.

I will deceive the *Christos* into seeing his kingdom as primarily a physical one. I'll take advantage of his great hunger. Security through power and satisfying material needs will become more important than trusting and obeying the *Sender*. Self-gratification must become his immediate interest. Then I will dance with glee, for he will have repeated Israel's ancient sin of elevating lust for physical things above trust in the *Sender*. He will have become my ally.

So, you think you are God's Son? Well, if you really are, then prove it to yourself and to me by turning a few of these stones into bread?

Admittedly, I was unprepared for his answer.

"The Scriptures say clearly that 'man shall not live on bread alone.'"

Stinging failure! He has refused to repeat Israel's sin. Instead of taking matters into his own hands and pushing his own physical needs to the head of the list, he seems anxious to comply with the *Sender*'s will.

So, I must strike deeper than the physical. In a vision, I will transport him to a high place and show him the error of his ways.

The *Christos* is headed for some very dark times as he seeks to establish his kingdom. At first everything will seem rosy as his popularity flourishes. Almost everyone will speak well of him. The excitable masses will flock to hear his every word and see the miracles he will perform. But when they begin to understand what being his disciples requires, they will desert him en masse. Unspeakable suffering on a cross lies astride the path that leads to his kingdom. Pulling no punches, the *Christos* will tell his would-be disciples that the way of the cross will be theirs as well. When that sinks in, they will leave in a cloud of dust. Even his close disciples will peel away one by one.

I know a thing or two about setting up kingdoms; suffering on crosses isn't required. The best way to establish a kingdom is to accumulate power and resort to violence when necessary. I should know; I have tailored many of them.

The *Christos* must be instructed and diverted from his intended path. If he successfully follows the way of the cross and establishes a kingdom built on suffering love, then the world order I have so carefully crafted will crumble. High stakes; I will gladly give him all I have if he will change course.

I will now show him all I have to offer. The authority and glory I offer are far superior—and more accessible—than what the *Christos* can achieve through the cross. Adjust his primary loyalty a bit, and the kingdom can be obtained quickly and painlessly. Adjust the *Sender*'s plan a bit here and there, and grab the power needed to operate—that is how we play the game.

"Tell you what I am willing to do. I already have authority over the kingdoms of this world. I can give power, success, and fame to whomsoever I please. You say you want a kingdom? I can arrange it. In fact, if you will but worship me, I will give you all the kingdoms you can handle—all the kingdoms of the world!"

Not since the days of Adam and Eve have I been so shamefully rebuked! "You are an ancient liar and a deceiver. Worship belongs not to you but to the Lord God alone. Only he is to be worshipped." What an answer!

He seems determined to do what I refused to do and what most of Adam's children since have refused to do: worship the *Sender* alone. Even if obedience leads to the cross—and even in the face of my fiercest opposition—the *Christos* is bent on obeying the *Sender*. He is determined to make all allegiances, attractions, and motivations serve his Father's will and glory.

The threat the *Christos* poses is alarming.

Fearing things might reach this point, I have held my most powerful weapon in reserve. I cannot dissuade him from pursuing the *Sender*'s will. So I must make him think he is worshipping the *Sender* when in fact he is worshipping himself. The *Christos* uses Scripture; so will I.

In a vision, I will take him to a high place on the temple—a good place to quote the Bible.

I have chosen a psalm. It tells how the *Sender* looks after those whom he shelters. I have succeeded in making many of his followers believe that's what the *Sender* is all about—shielding his people against all threats. That's the purpose, they think, for his existence. I have made them believe that in exchange for serving the *Sender* they get to dictate what "divine protection" means. If the *Sender* doesn't satisfy their expectations, they can indict his faithfulness. These people never seem to understand (this is my secret) that by dictating to the *Sender* they reverse roles with him: they become "all-wise gods" and he the "obedient servant." Foolish people, they are but functional atheists disguised as Christians. My intrigue succeeds repeatedly—produces large groups who think they are worshipping the *Sender* when in fact they are worshipping themselves.

Now I'll create a situation in which the *Christos* will dictate the terms under which the *Sender* can prove his faithfulness. The Conspiracy will succeed.

If you really are God's Son, then he ought to be willing to satisfy your desires and protect you from harm. There's a good way to find out if that's true. Jump off this pinnacle. If God saves you, then he really is your Father and you are his Son— simple enough. After all, don't the Scriptures promise that God will dispatch angels to protect you, even to keep you from tripping over a rock?

CATASTROPHE LOOMS!

The *Christos* didn't "bite." He refused to put the *Sender* to the test—said his character and history are sufficient. He quoted Scripture: "Don't tell God how to be God, and don't tell him what he must do to win your approval!" He said what I was demanding would only demonstrate a lack of trust in the *Sender*. It would also show doubt about his competence and dependability.

I am dismayed! The *Christos* seems perfectly willing to let the *Sender* be the *Sender* on his own terms—trust without testing.

However, I will not give up! My seeming defeat is but temporary. Fight remains. . . . I will return.

I will convince his disciples to undercut his mission by accepting my offers.

A *FIELD MANUAL* FOR DEFEATING THE BAAL CONSPIRACY

The New Testament uses a variety of ways to describe the wealth of spiritual resources the Father has given the Church. God graces the Church with his riches for numerous reasons. One is preparation for battle against the Chief Conspirator and his allies. Though boisterous and threatening, Satan is an inferior and sentenced foe. On two occasions, Jesus spoke of judgment coming upon the "prince of this world" (John 12:31; 16:11, NIV).

The New Testament suffers no illusions about the enemy's goals. The kingdom of evil is real, and it is sworn to subvert God's kingdom. Jesus spoke of "an enemy" planting weeds in Jesus' field, hoping to ruin his harvest (Matt. 13:24-30).

But the New Testament's realism doesn't leave informed Christians biting their nails. Christ has given the Church abundant resources for the conflict at hand (Col. 2:8-15; Rev. 12:9-12). In a parabolic statement, Jesus said it takes a "stronger man" to bind a "strong man" and plunder his property. Jesus is the "stronger man" and Satan is the "strong man" (see Mark 3:20-27; Col. 2:15). The Baal Conspiracy can succeed only in persons who do not radically align themselves with the "stronger man."

Promises fairly tumble from the pages of the New Testament. "In [Christ] every one of God's promises is a 'Yes.' For this reason it is through him that we say the 'Amen,' to the glory of God" (2 Cor. 1:20). "Greater is he that is in you, than he that is in the world" (1 John 4:4, KJV). The powers of darkness will not be able to withstand a Church fully armed with the Holy Spirit (Matt. 16:18). "You are a chosen race, a royal priesthood, a holy nation, God's own people, that you may declare the wonderful deeds of him who called you out of darkness into his marvelous light" (1 Pet. 2:9, RSV).

The Baal Conspiracy feeds on deception and perversion of God's good gifts. It is parasitical, having no life of its own. When confronted by the light of the gospel and the power of the Holy Spirit, it retreats—just as shadows flee from the rising sun.

Just as the New Testament boldly proclaims the Father's promises, it also openly calls for unrelenting discipleship. The two are inseparable. All Christians are offered full access to the Savior's riches. There are no elites in his kingdom. Christ's storehouse is open to all who refuse to dabble on the edges of obedience. The gospel train leaves behind only those who linger at the ticket booth arguing over the fare.

In this chapter we will concentrate on the Epistle to the Ephesians as a *field manual* to be used to defeat the Baal Conspiracy—by each of us and by the Church. The *manual* contains four sections: (1) worship: the point of departure; (2) Christ the Victor; (3) the Church; and (4) deployment for battle.

Ephesians eloquently states how richly Christ has endowed his Church. It also masterfully announces a call to diligent discipleship

Many scholars believe Ephesians was originally a circular letter distributed to numerous congregations. Somehow, the copy the church at Ephesus possessed found its way into the New Testament. So, in a special sense, the letter is addressed to all Christians.

The Epistle brims with confidence in Christ and his Church. It is an extended doxology, a glorification of the triune God. One of its brief doxologies expresses the whole: "Now to him who by the power at work within us is able to accomplish abundantly far more than all we can ask or imagine, to him be glory in the church and in Christ Jesus to all generations, forever and ever. Amen" (3:20-21).

Let's examine how this *field manual* prepares Christians to defeat the Baal Conspiracy.

WORSHIP: THE INDISPENSABLE POINT OF DEPARTURE

Ephesians is distinct in its use of superlatives. Apparently, the writer thought that when speaking of God a frugal use of language was inadequate. Simply saying "the riches of the Father's inheritance" or "God's power" was not enough. He felt compelled to add "glorious" to "inheritance" and "greatness" to "power" (Eph. 1:18-19). In coming ages, the Father will not simply demonstrate the "riches of his grace," he will show "the immeasurable riches of his grace" (2:7).

However, the Epistle doesn't begin by concentrating on the "glorious inheritance" Christians have received. It begins in worship. "Blessed be the God and Father of our Lord Jesus Christ, who has blessed us in Christ" (1:3). Each blessing the Father gives occurs "according to the good pleasure of his will" and "to the praise of his glorious grace that he freely bestowed on us in the Beloved" (vv. 5-6). The Epistle's controlling center is worship of the *sovereign God* who reveals himself *through* the riches of his grace. Everything is placed in the context of worship.

Why is this so important? Because unless we begin by worshipping God *just because of who he is* and not *because* of his blessings, we will open doors through which the Baal Conspiracy can enter. The Conspiracy began by refusing to worship God as God. Its devices and intrigues simply continue the ancient refusal. Christians who treat worship of God as something he "earns" and as a "reward" for his services play into the hands of the Conspiracy.

God does not "earn" our worship; he *manifests his glory,* his *Godness,* in the riches he bestows. Our first response should be worship—doxology. His many gifts are the *means through which* we worship him, not the *reasons* we worship him. They are occasions for worship. Through his gifts, God *declares his Name* in all creation.

Ephesians teaches us that the eternal God is worthy of worship before he "gives" anything. True, he is "for us," but he is also "above us." He is not "separated from us," but he is God "before" and "apart from us."

God's *holiness* means his "Godness"—his absolute singularity as God. He asks, "To whom then will you compare me, or who is my equal? . . . Have you not known? Have you not heard? The LORD is the everlasting God, the Creator of the ends of the earth" (Isa. 40:25, 28). Moses sang, "Who is like you, majestic in holiness, awesome in splendor" (Exod. 15:11).

God's *glory* means the active manifestation—the going forth, the overflow—of his holiness. Because of the history of God's creative and redemptive deeds—definitively revealed "in the Beloved"—we know that his "going forth" is the "going forth" of grace. In his presence we cry, "Holy, holy, holy is the LORD of hosts; the whole earth is full of his glory" (Isa. 6:1-3).

God's *righteousness* is the active manifestation of the *moral content* of his holiness (Ps. 9:8; 11:7; Jer. 9:24). To say that God acts in righteousness means that he faithfully "does" himself, not that he measures up to some moral standard standing above him. The Bible rejoices that God is faithful to himself and hence faithful to his people (Ps. 40:10; 89:5; Lam. 3:23; Luke 1:46-55; 2 Cor. 1:18-22). He keeps covenant, lets the oppressed go free, acts in steadfast love, judges justly, corrects oppression, defends the fatherless, and pleads for the widow.

Worship includes asking God to reproduce his righteousness in us so we can glorify him. Paul urged the Roman Christians to be "transformed by the renewing of [their] minds, so that [they] may discern what is the will of God—what is good and acceptable and perfect" (Rom. 12:2). Paul says that such transformation expresses our "worship" of God (v. 1). Ephesians says that we have been called "to live for the praise of [God's] glory" (1:12, RSV).

New Testament theologian Ben Witherington offers a summary: "Believers are saved in order to serve, saved in order to model the character of God to the world, saved in order to worship the one true God."[5]

CHRIST THE VICTOR

The second major feature of our *field manual* demonstrates how one-sided the battle against the Baal Conspiracy is. The *manual* doesn't minimize the threat we face. It confronts the Conspiracy's "unfruitful works of darkness" head on (Eph. 5:11). In full disclosure, Ephesians warns that our struggle is not "against flesh and blood, but against the principalities, against the powers, against the world rulers of this present darkness, against the spiritual hosts of wickedness in the heavenly places" (6:12, RSV). But as dangerous as the Baal Conspiracy might be, its future already has been sealed by our Lord. He "was crucified also for us under Pontius Pilate; he suffered and was buried; and the third day he rose again according to the Scriptures, and ascended into heaven, and sitteth on the right hand of the Father; and he shall come again, with glory, to judge both the quick and the dead; whose kingdom shall have no end" (Nicene Creed).[6]

Who is this Christ?

He is the eternal Son in and through whom the Father of glory freely bestowed his riches. Why? Just because he wanted to! "In him we have redemption through his blood, the forgiveness of our trespasses, according to the riches of his grace that he lavished on us" (Eph. 1:7-8). Let's not think of God's grace as a substance to be hoarded and stored. Instead, it is the Father's glorious and active presence in the Church in the person of the living Christ. He is "above . . . and through . . . and in" its members (4:6). The Father gives himself to us according to the measure of Christ, the Church's head—a "measure" already paradoxically described as "immeasurable" (vv. 6-7).

What does the Father intend to accomplish through his Son?

In Christ he intends to "gather up all things in him, things in heaven and things on earth" (1:10). He is redeeming his creation; he is *recapitulating* (gathering back) to the Father what sin has *alienated*. In this age, and in ages to come, the Father will continue to compound "his grace in kindness toward us in Christ Jesus" (2:7). This gives us a peek into what heaven will be—riches piled on riches.

The lavish redemption the Father inaugurated in Christ is a cosmic demonstration of his "immeasurable" greatness and power (1:19). Think of it! On Easter morn, the same divine power that brought the world into existence—from the spinning nebulae to cellular life—focused on Jesus' rock-hewn tomb and raised him from the dead. He who bore the weight of the world's sin was then elevated to the Father's right hand (v. 20). From there he exercises authority over "all rule and authority and power and dominion" (v. 21). Not content with that, the Father has made him to rule over "every name that is named, not only in this age but also in the age to come" (v. 21).

Next, in place of the old fallen humanity, Christ has become the Head, the Author, of a new humanity. He accomplished this through his faithful obedience to the Father—even to death on the cross (see Phil. 2:8). The new humanity is created "according to the likeness of God in true righteousness and holiness" (Eph. 4:24).

The unbroken faith and uncompromised worship the Son demonstrated can now characterize those who are his sisters and brothers. Notice that Christ did not set out to show how Gentiles might be included in the old covenant. He created a completely new humanity (2:15-16) that transcends the old distinctions. The *Epistle to Diognetus*—a beautiful late second-century expression of Christian piety—even says that a "new race or way of life has appeared on earth."[7] In place of the designation "stranger to the household of God" (see Eph. 2:19), Christ has made us fellow citizens, fellow heirs, sharers of the promises with the saints (see 2:19; 3:6).

Was this some new idea that popped into God's mind during his long journey with the Jews? Did he fail in his sojourn with them? Not at all. Christ is the fulfillment of what the Father had in mind all along. Long before the world was created, the Father "blessed us in Christ" by appointing him to become author of a people who would be "holy and blameless before [the Father] in love" (Eph. 1:3-4; Titus 2:11-14). In his incarnate and ever-obedient Son, the Father carried out his eternal purpose—a "mystery" that had been "hidden for ages" (Eph. 3:9). When all the historical factors had matured, God acted in a way no one could have precisely anticipated: he revealed his mystery—his plan to create a new humanity, a new Adam, in Jesus Christ. The old skins could not contain the new wine (Matt.

9:17; Mark 2:22). The prophets anticipated the grace that would one day be ours through Jesus. Even the angels longed to look into the mystery, but could not (1 Pet. 1:12). Jesus said many prophets and righteous men longed to see and hear the kingdom of God (Matt. 13:16-17; Luke 10:23-24). Revelation of the mystery was reserved for Christ's Church.

The Father will do even more. He will, through the Church's witness, declare his wise plan of redemption even to the "rulers and authorities in the heavenly places," that is, to the rich variety of angelic beings (Eph. 3:10). No wonder the writer became so overwhelmed he paused and bowed his knees to God in worship (v. 14).

> *Worship, honor, power, and blessing*
> *thou art worthy to receive;*
> *highest praises, without ceasing,*
> *right it is for us to give.*
> *Help, ye bright angelic spirits,*
> *all your noblest anthems raise;*
> *help to sing our Savior's merits,*
> *help to chant Emmanuel's praise.*

(John Bakewell, 1721—1819; Martin Madan, 1726-90)[8]

GOD WILL HAVE A PEOPLE: THE ROLE OF THE CHURCH IN DEFEATING THE BAAL CONSPIRACY

The Epistle to the Ephesians is a "Church Epistle." It lets us know that God places the Church front and center in the battle against the Baal Conspiracy. The success of one means the defeat of the other. With so much riding on the Church, the reason for Satan's urgent and persistent opposition to it becomes clear.

The importance of the Church in God's plan, as Ephesians describes it, is strange territory for many of us. We tend to see the Church as less pivotal than we should. To understand God's strategy for defeating the Baal Conspiracy we will need to listen with fresh ears and be ready to make some important adjustments.

Here is what Ephesians teaches. Unless the triune God can successfully create a people—right here in the middle of his creation—defined by his own character and life, he will face defeat as Creator and Redeemer and must withdraw from the field of battle. Scholars tell us the essential meaning of God's creation of Eve as Adam's companion is that God created the conditions for harmonious community. Sadly, sin disrupted all that (Gen. 2:4*b*—3:24). In one book after another the Bible tracks the Conspiracy's efforts to block God's love made manifest in community.

Had a way to heal that disruption not been found, God would have failed to bear witness to himself *in* his creation. Why? Because community is essential to God's own life as Father, Son, and Holy Spirit—One God, blessed forever. Theologians use the word *perichoresis* (peri-ko-rē-sis) to describe the mutual indwelling (mutual self-giving) of the Father, Son, and Holy Spirit. God as love is the source and quality of that mutual self-giving. An important feature of the New Testament is that the Father, Son, and Holy Spirit most often bear witness to each other, not to themselves (e.g., John 14—17).

For God to be truly proclaimed and known in heaven and on earth there *must be* a people that reflect his own life. The love and mutual self-giving that characterize God's life must somehow mark that community. They must be empowered to give themselves to each other with a love that is God's love.

The New Testament says the Church of Jesus Christ is that community. It is the new and true Israel of God. How did such a community come to be? The Church was created and is now sustained by the Father, through the atoning Son, and in the power of the Holy Spirit. For this reason, it is the Church of God. It is the field in which God has planted and invested himself—staked his reputation. It is nurtured by the Holy Spirit and will bear fruit "according to the likeness of God in true righteousness and holiness" (Eph. 4:24).

Without such a people God would have to yield his creation to the Baal Conspiracy—to chaos. It would not be enough for him to redeem isolated individuals. They could never testify to the triune God who is love; they could never reflect his unity. They might succeed in forming temporary, incidental associations, but they could never be community as God is "Community."

Modern individualism has played havoc with our understanding of the Church. We have been conditioned to think of individual Christians as primary, and the Church as secondary—like so many terminals connected directly to Jesus the Super Computer. The Church is often viewed as a relatively inconsequential afterthought. When someone challenges this way of thinking, we Protestants often reply that we "don't want to be Roman Catholics." But the New Testament witness about the Church stands firm.

According to Ephesians we can be "in" Christ only as parts of his Body—the Church. "Lone Christians" is a contradictory phrase. In the Church, as nowhere else, the Father is manifesting his Name, his Glory. It plays an essential role in fulfilling the mystery of redemption.

Listen to what Ephesians says about the Church.

1. God put the immeasurable greatness of his power to work in the resurrection of Jesus, placed him at his right hand, and "made him head over all things." He did this "for the Church" (1:22).

2. What *is* the Church?

The Church *is* the "body" of the risen and reigning Christ (5:22-24). He nourishes and tenderly cares for his Body. He unashamedly identifies with it (vv. 25-33).

The Church *is* the "fullness of [Christ] who fills all in all" (1:22-23). We may say that it is the *fullness* of *the Fullness.* Downgrading the church's importance would require downgrading Christ himself.

The Church *is* the "household of God." Gentiles who were "far off" and Jews who were "near" have become members of God's household. They have become citizens of his kingdom through the Holy Spirit (2:15-19). Now "there is one body and one Spirit, just as you were called to the one hope of your calling, one Lord, one faith, one baptism, one God and Father of all, who is above all and through all and in all" (4:4-6).

The Church *is* the "holy temple" of God, built upon the foundation of the apostles and prophets. Christ is its cornerstone. Christians are its interlocking parts ("members of one another" [4:25; 5:21]). Even now we can see the "holy temple" taking shape. What will the completed structure be? "A dwelling place for God" (2:22).

3. Christ has given active roles to all his disciples for achieving the Church's *fullness* and hence his *Fullness.* The roles come to us as gifts to be used for "building up the body of Christ" until it reaches "the full stature of Christ" (4:7-16).

Let the Church rejoice and the Baal Conspiracy tremble at these descriptions of the Church and Christ's gifts to us. The glory of God who by his sovereign power accomplishes more than "we can ask or imagine" is manifesting himself in Christ Jesus and in his Church. For how long will this go on? "To all generations, forever and ever. Amen" (3:20-21).

THE GREAT DEPLOYMENT

Lest we end prematurely in exultation, hear a parable. On January 27, 1862, President Abraham Lincoln ordered the Union Army under General George B. McClellan to begin a unified aggressive action against the Confederate States of America. McClellan ignored the president's order. He said his army was not yet ready to confront the Confederates. He responded this way though he had raised a well-trained, well-supplied, and well-organized army. He outnumbered his enemy but repeatedly overestimated its strength. McClellan always seemed to need more time, more men, and more preparations. He was a brilliant engineer and a highly capable organizer. He just didn't seem to have a stomach for battle. Lincoln said, "If General McClellan does not want to use the army, I would like to borrow it for a time." Eventually, under orders from the War Department, on November 9, 1862, McClellan relinquished command and returned to his home in Trenton, New Jersey, never to be asked to command an army again.

Despite all the "immeasurable riches" Christ has given to us, if all we do is "march," and don't get around to deploying aggressively his resources against the Baal Conspiracy, we should not be surprised if the Lord hands the "command" to someone else (Matt. 25:14-30).

The Epistle to the Ephesians doesn't neglect training, but it doesn't stop there. It commands, "Engage!" Forcefully engage the Chief Conspirator and his agents wherever they are found. There is only one acceptable outcome: total victory. To borrow the words of Winston Churchill, the Epistle seems to say, "We shall fight on the seas and oceans, we shall fight with growing confidence and growing strength in the air. . . . We shall fight on the beaches, we shall fight on the landing grounds, we shall

fight in the fields and in the streets, we shall fight in the hills.
. . ."[9] Unlike the British whose resources for fighting the Nazis were marginal, Christ supplies unlimited resources to his people. Observe the supply list (italics added):

- "According to the purpose of him who *accomplishes* all things according to the counsel of his will" (Eph. 1:11, RSV).
- You "have been *brought near* in the blood of Christ" (2:13, RSV).
- You "[he] *made . . . alive* together with Christ . . . and *raised [you] up* with him" (vv. 5-6, RSV).
- You have been "*sealed* with the promised Holy Spirit, which is the guarantee of our inheritance until we *acquire* possession of it, to the praise of his glory" (1:13-14, RSV).
- May the Father of glory "*give* you a spirit of wisdom and of revelation in the knowledge of him" (v. 17, RSV).
- "That you may *know* what is the hope to which he has called you" (v. 18, RSV).
- "That through the church the manifold wisdom of God might now *be made known*" (3:10, RSV).
- "According to the riches of his glory he may *grant* you to be *strengthened* with might through his Spirit" (v. 16, RSV).

Against such resources the Baal Conspiracy is helpless. But they must be deployed in battle, not just held in reserve.

Let's now receive the Lord's commission for engaging the Conspiracy:

In conclusion be strong—not in yourselves but in the Lord, in the power of his boundless strength. Put on God's complete armour so that you can successfully resist all the devil's craftiness. For our fight is not against any physical enemy: it is against organisations and powers that are spiritual. We are up against the unseen power that controls this dark world, and spiritual agents from the very headquarters of evil. Therefore you must wear the whole armour of God that you may be able to resist evil in its day of power, and even when you have fought to a standstill you may still stand your ground. Take your stand then with truth as your belt, integrity your breastplate, the gospel of peace firmly on your feet, salvation as your helmet and in your hand the sword of the Spirit, the Word of God. Above all be sure you take faith as your shield, for it can quench every burning missile the enemy hurls at you. In all your petitions pray at all times with every kind of spiritual prayer, keeping alert and persistent as you pray for all Christ's men and women. And pray for me, too, that I may be able to speak the message here boldly, to make known the secret of that gospel for which I am an ambassador in chains. Pray that I may speak out about it as is my plain and obvious duty. (Eph. 6:10-20, PHILLIPS)

There are no "McClellans" in the text!

> *Did we in our own strength confide,*
> *Our striving would be losing,*
> *Were not the right Man on our side,*
> *The Man of God's own choosing.*
> *Dost ask who that may be?*
> *Christ Jesus, it is He;*
> *Lord Sabaoth, His name;*
> *From age to age the same,*
> *And He must win the battle.*

(Martin Luther, 1483—1546)[10]

A TIMELINE

Division of the United Kingdom after the death of Solomon	—	ca. 922 BC
Ahab (king of Israel)	—	ca. 869-850
Elijah	—	ca. 850
Jeroboam II (king of Israel)	—	ca. 786-750
Amos	—	ca. 750
Hosea	—	ca. 745
Micah	—	ca. 722-ca. 701
Fall of Israel	—	722-721
Hezekiah (king of Judah)	—	ca. 715—687
Josiah (king of Judah)	—	640-609
Jehoiakim (Josiah's son)	—	609—598
Jeremiah	—	ca. 626—587
First deportation to Babylon	—	598/7
Fall of Jerusalem and second deportation to Babylon	—	587
Babylonian Exile	—	597-ca. 538
Return of the exiles, rebuilding the temple, Ezra and Nehemiah	—	520—ca. 398 (?)
Birth of Jesus	—	ca. 6-4 BC (based upon an erroneous dating of Rome's founding)
Paul ministers in Corinth	—	ca. AD 50-52

NOTES

1. G. K. Beale, *We Become What We Worship: A Biblical Theology of Idolatry* (Downers Grove, Ill.: IVP Academic, 2008), 21.

2. Alister McGrath, *Dawkins' God: Genes, Memes, and the Meaning of Life* (Malden, Mass.: Blackwell Publishing, 2005).

3. Dietrich Bonhoeffer, *The Cost of Discipleship* (London: SCM Press, 1948), 41-56.

4. Dennis Bratcher, e-mail response to author's question, March 3, 2008.

5. Ben Witherington, *The Indelible Image: The Theological and Ethical Thought World of the New Testament*, vol. 1, *The Individual Witnesses* (Downers Grove, Ill.: IVP Academic, 2009), 230.

6. *Book of Common Prayer* (New York: Church Hymnal Corporation, 1979), 328.

7. "The So-called Letter to Diognetus," (Grand Rapids: Christian Classics Ethereal Library), http://www.ccel.org/ccel/richardson/fathers.x.i.ii.html (accessed March 4, 2010).

8. *The Hymnal 1982: According to the Use of the Episcopal Church* (New York: Church Hymnal Corporation, 1985), 495.

9. Winston Churchill, War Situation, 4 June 1940, House of Commons Debates (TheyWorkForYou.com), http://www.theyworkforyou.com/debates/?id=1940-06-04a.787.0 (accessed March 4, 2010).

10. Martin Luther, "A Mighty Fortress Is Our God," *Sing to the Lord* (Kansas City: Lillenas Publishing Co., 1993), 30.